Eighty-four Āsanas in Yoga

A Survey of Traditions

(with Illustrations)

Eighty-four Āsanas in Yoga
A Survey of Traditions
(with Illustrations)

Gudrun Bühnemann

PRINTWORLD
Publishers of Indian Traditions

Cataloging in Publication Data — DK
[Courtesy: D.K. Agencies (P) Ltd. <docinfo@dkagencies.com>]

Bühnemann, Gudrun, author.
Eighty-four āsanas in yoga : a survey of traditions : with illustrations / Gudrun Bühnemann. – Fourth impression.
pages cm
"First published in India in 2007" – Title page verso.
Includes bibliographical references and index.
ISBN 9788124604175 (Hb)
ISBN 9788124605806 (Pb)

1. Hatha yoga – History I. Title.

LCC BL1238.56.H38B85 2021 | DDC 613.7046 23

ISBN 978-81-246-0417-5 (Hb)
ISBN 978-81-246-0580-6 (Pb)
First published in India in 2007
Second impression, 2011, Third impression, 2016
Fourth impression, 2021

Printed and published by:
D.K. Printworld (P) Ltd.
Regd. office : *'Vedaśrī,'* F-395, Sudarshan Park
(Metro Station: Ramesh Nagar)
New Delhi - 110 015
Phones: (011) 2545 3975, 2546 6019; *Fax*: (011) 2546 5926
E-mail: indology@dkprintworld.com
Web: www.dkprintworld.com

Contents

Acknowledgements

I would like to thank Professor R. Linrothe for kindly making his photographs of selected murals in Mahāmandir available for reproduction in this book and for providing useful information and comments regarding Siddha traditions.

I am grateful to the British Library, London, for granting permission to reproduce the coloured drawings of the eighty-four *āsanas* from manuscript Add. 24099. I am especially thankful to Dr. J.P. Losty, Dr. D. Wujastyk and Dr. E. de Michelis for their help in connection with this manuscript. The Center for South Asia and the Graduate School of the University of Wisconsin-Madison have generously contributed to meeting the high cost of ordering the images.

I wish to thank the authorities of the Keśar Library, Kathmandu, for permitting me to reproduce the drawings of *āsanas* from colour photocopies of manuscript 347.

I am indebted to Dr. Lokesh Chandra for sending photocopies of the drawings of the eighty-four Siddhas according to the Jodhpur tradition (referred to as N1), which are reproduced in this book, and to Dr. N.E. Sjoman for providing photocopies of an identical set of drawings from another publication (referred to as N2) for comparison's sake.

I wish to thank A. Sanchez and S. Wong/Sanchez for permission to reproduce the photographs of the eighty-four *āsanas* in the Yoga Challenge® system from a poster published in 2003.

I am grateful to the late Dr. M.L. Gharote for supplying several textual references and responding to my questions regarding the texts he edited, to Professor K.S. Arjunwadkar for suggestions on an earlier draft of this book and to Professors D.G. White, C.W. Ernst and J. Bautze and to G.J.R. Mevissen, M.A., for providing some useful information.

Finally, I thank Dr. M. Palangat of the University of Wisconsin-Madison for providing a reading of the names of the eighty-four *āsanas* written in Malayalam script and listed in Appendix 8.4 and P. Pierce, M.A., for editing this book for English style.

Guide to Transliteration and Pronunciation

In this book Sanskrit and Hindī words are transliterated according to the standard system used by Indologists. Exceptions are some names of places and persons written in their most common anglicized forms without diacritical marks.

Long vowels are the dipthongs *e*, *o*, *ai* and *au* and vowels marked with a macron; all other vowels are short.

a is pronounced like the *u* in b*u*t
ā like the *a* in c*a*r
i like the *i* in h*i*t
ī like the *ī* in mach*i*ne
u like the *u* in p*u*t
ū like the *u* in r*u*le
ṛ like the *ri* in *ri*ff
e like the *ay* in p*ay*
ai like the *ai* in *ai*sle
o like the *o* in l*o*w
au like the *ow* in h*ow*.

The *ṃ* nasalizes the preceding vowel; it may also be pronounced like the English *m*.

Consonants are divided into aspirated consonants written with a following *h* (for example, *kh*) and unaspirated ones (for example, *k*). The retroflex sounds *ṭ*, *ṭh*, etc. are pronounced with the tip of the tongue turned back and touching the upper palate. The letter *g* is always hard and pronounced like the *g* in *g*oat. The letter *c* is pronounced as in *ch*in. The *ṅ* is pronounced like the *ng* in ri*ng*; *ñ* sounds like the Spanish *ñ* in se*ñ*ora. The palatal sibilant *ś* and the retroflex *ṣ* sound similar to English *sh*.

List of Illustrations

1. The Coloured Drawings of the Āsanas according to the Jogapradīpakā

This is a circa nineteenth-century set of drawings of eighty-four *āsanas* illustrating a section of Jayatarāma's Jogapradīpakā. The set is part of a document containing coloured drawings of eighty-four *āsanas* and twenty-four *mudrās*, each accompanied by text. The document was removed from the library of the Rānī of Jhansi in central India in 1858 and has been kept in the British Library since 1861, where it is catalogued as manuscript Add. 24099. The document is described in section 6.2.1, the drawings of the *āsanas* are reproduced in section 6.2.2 and the names of the *āsanas* are listed in Appendix 8.2.

2. The Line Drawings from Nepal

This is a set of line drawings showing practitioners performing *āsanas*, numbered from one to eighty-four. The drawings form part of manuscript 347 preserved in the Keśar Library, Kathmandu. The manuscript consists of forty-eight folios and is labelled "Hastamudrā, caurāshī āsana," which means 'hand gestures, eighty-four *āsanas*.' The section on *āsanas* consists of fifteen folios. The manuscript is described in section 6.3.1 and the line drawings are reproduced in section 6.3.2.

3. The Sources in the Jodhpur Tradition

3a. This is a set of line drawings of the eighty-four Siddhas performing eighty-four Yoga postures, reproduced from the Appendix (pp. 1–21) of the book "Nava nātha caurāsī siddha" compiled by Yogin Naraharinātha and published by the Gorakṣanātha Maṭha (Vārāṇasī) in 1968. The line drawings are copies of older drawings in the Jodhpur style. The copies were made by Prabhātnāth Yogī of the Division for the Propagation of Yoga (*yogapracāriṇī śākhā*) of the (Śrī) Siddha Ratnanāth Arts Institute (Kalā Kendra) at Caugharā in the Dāṅ district of western Nepal in 1968. The line drawings are described in section 6.4.1 and reproduced in section 6.4.2.

3b. These are selected portraits of individual Siddhas performing different *āsana*s which decorate the walls of the sanctum of the large temple at the Mahāmandir temple complex outside Jodhpur, in central Rājasthān. The construction of this Nātha temple was completed under Mān Singh, the Mahārāja of Marwar, in 1805. The murals possibly date from 1810. The sixteen portraits correspond to line drawings 1, 4, 11, 21, 25, 32, 34, 46, 50, 53, 58, 60, 64, 65, 68 and 71. The portraits are described in section 6.4.3 and reproduced in section 6.4.4. The photographs were taken by R. Linrothe who kindly made them available for publication in this book.

4. The Line Drawings in Svāmī Svayamānanda 1992

These are contemporary line drawings of eighty-four *āsana*s reproduced from Svāmī Svayamānanda 1992. The line drawings are described in section 5.4.3 and reproduced in section 6.5. The *āsana* names are listed in Appendix 8.5.

5. Photographs of the Eighty-four Āsanas in the Yoga Challenge® System

These are photographs of the eighty-four *āsana*s taught by A. Sanchez as part of Yoga Challenge® IV. They are reproduced from a poster published in 2003. The *āsana*s are described in section 5.4.4, their names listed in Appendix 8.6 and the photographs reproduced in section 6.6.

List of Tables

Frequently Used Abbreviations

GS Gheraṇḍa-Saṃhitā.

GŚ Gorakṣaśataka.

HP1 Haṭhapradīpikā. The Haṭhayogapradīpikā of Svātmārāma with the Commentary Jyotsnā of Brahmānanda and English Translation. Adyar, Madras: Adyar Library and Research Centre, 1975 (reprint of 1972).

HP2 Haṭhapradīpikā. Haṭhapradīpikā (with 10 Chapters) of Svātmārāma. With Yoga-prakāśikā Commentary by Bālakṛṣṇa. Edited by M.L. Gharote and P. Devnath. Lonavla: The Lonavla Yoga Institute, 2001.

HR1 Haṭharatnāvalī. Hatharatnavali of Srinivasabhatta Mahayogindra. Editor: M. Venkata Reddy. Secunderabad: M. Ramakrishna Reddy, 1982.

HR2 Haṭharatnāvalī. Haṭharatnāvalī (A Treatise on haṭhayoga) of Śrīnivāsayogī. Critically edited by M.L. Gharote/P. Devnath/V.K. Jha. Lonavla: The Lonavla Yoga Institute, 2002.

JP Jogapradīpakā.

N1 Nava nātha caurāsī siddha. <Compiled> by Yogī Naraharinātha. Vārāṇasī: Gorakṣanātha Maṭha, 1968 (in Hindī).

N2 Nava nātha caurāsī siddha bālāsundarī yogamāyā. Puṇe: Akhila Bhāratavarṣīya Yoga-pracāriṇī Mahāsabhā Prakāśanam, 1968 (in Marāṭhī).

ŚS Śiva-Saṃhitā.

YS Yogasūtra(s).

1. Introduction

Physical postures (*āsana*) are the most important and often the only constituent of modern Yoga. Many practitioners believe that the postures derive from an ancient original set of eighty-four *āsanas*. In this book I trace, for the first time, traditions of eighty-four postures by examining original materials, including line drawings, descriptions in older Indic texts and modern publications which reflect contemporary traditions. I have also taken up a number of broader issues related to the topic of Yoga postures so as to provide the reader with a larger context. At the same time I see this as a welcome opportunity to summarize for a wider public the results of comparatively new academic research on Yoga.

How can one define Yoga? Yoga is often popularly considered to be a single unified system. However, under the term Yoga can be subsumed a diverse body of teachings and a variety of practices and approaches, which were traditionally passed on from teacher to student and then codified in texts. Definitions of Yoga necessarily vary with schools and systems, and no one comprehensive definition of Yoga can be given.[1] Literal translations of the term Yoga include 'union' and 'means,' among others.

A common characteristic of many traditional Yoga systems is a structured approach, which consists of a set of prescribed practices, often arranged in graded components. The disciple progresses through a sequence of practices with the help of a teacher to a goal, which in most cases is defined as liberation from the cycle of existence (*saṃsāra*) and/or union with a deity or divine principle. In most systems a set of moral precepts and rules of conduct are ordained so as to provide a foundation for practice. The final state is often defined as meditative absorption (*samādhi*). Components of Yoga practice often include dietary restrictions; cultivating a balanced mind and an attitude of indifference to pairs of opposites, which are defined as heat/cold, pleasure/pain, and so forth; and solitary meditation. Measurable signs of progress, which signal the practitioner's success, are described in the texts. These include physical changes and visions, among other things. Yoga differs from the varied ancient Indian practice of austerities which mortify the body, since it emphasizes a balanced and controlled approach that avoids extremes.

In recent years Yoga has become decontextualized, commercialized and transformed into a mass movement in Western culture, where it has been made into a practice to enhance physical fitness and beauty—often labelled as *haṭhayoga.*[2] This Western approach to Yoga has in turn influenced the way in which Yoga is now taught and practised in India, where one can witness the same traits that manifest themselves when traditional religious systems are adapted by people who practise them outside of their original contexts. It is evident that the Western and modern Indian concept of Yoga and the traditional Indian Yoga systems are not the same in nature and goal. One might in fact wonder whether the use of the term Yoga is appropriate for the former.

A common element of modern Yoga practice is the performance of postures. Some of the postures are shared by almost all modern schools, although the style of performance, such as the technique and speed, may again vary. The selection, number and sequence of postures practised vary greatly with traditions. A number frequently invoked as authentic by ancient and modern authorities is eighty-four. However, nothing is known about an original set of eighty-four *āsana*s. Despite the broad popular interest in Yoga and the growing number of publications on the subject, hardly any research has been done on the history of the practices which are often subsumed under the name *haṭhayoga*. With this book I hope to make a contribution to the subject by inquiring into traditions of eighty-four classical or basic postures. As a general introduction to the topic, a brief survey of relevant Yoga texts is provided below. Then the terms *haṭhayoga* and *rājayoga* are examined in some detail, since their meaning in the past differs greatly from author to author and is not as clear-cut as their modern usage. This is followed by a discussion of the place and function of *āsana*s in different Yoga systems. Then the number of *āsana*s in Yoga systems is examined, and several sets of eighty-four *āsana*s are presented from both older and modern sources. Most important among the pictorial representations are the coloured drawings according to

---

[1] A list of definitions of the term Yoga from Sanskrit texts can be found in Daniélou 1949: 6–8; definitions from other texts could easily be added to it.

[2] For a recent study of 'Modern (Postural) Yoga,' see Michelis 2004. The author also provides a detailed discussion of 'Neo-Haṭhayoga.' For Yoga in modern India, see also Alter 2004.

the Jogapradīpakā which are preserved in the British Library. They are of high artistic value and unique in that no other comparable illustrated manuscript has come to light so far. Among the sources illustrating sets of eighty-four postures, this manuscript therefore occupies a foremost position.

2. A Brief Survey of Relevant Texts

In this section I will introduce some important texts on Yoga referred to in this book, and their authors and dates as far as these are known. Dating material from South Asia is notoriously difficult. Large text passages were freely borrowed by compilers and inserted into new works. Passages from texts were also incorporated into works of anonymous Sanskrit literature such as the Purāṇas. The compilers' practice of extracting material from diverse sources frequently contributes to inconsistencies of thought and expression within one text. It is often difficult to decide which author borrowed from which and to establish a reliable chronology of texts. The fact that texts were also subjected to repeated redactions accounts for the fact that one text is often extant in several recensions of different length from different time periods—a problem which further complicates the dating of texts.

Several scholars have tried to find indications of early Yoga practice in seals of the Indus Valley civilization, but the evidence from that period is far from conclusive. Others have looked for elements of Yoga practice and early references to Yogins in the hymns of the Ṛgveda and Atharvaveda, but not much substantial material can be found. Teachings on Yoga appear first in passages of the earlier Upaniṣads. They are found in the Kaṭha-Upaniṣad (which dates from the last few centuries BCE), the Śvetāśvatara-Upaniṣad (the first two centuries CE?) and the Mokṣadharma section (roughly the early centuries CE) of the Mahābhārata, namely chapters 168–353 of the work's 12th book, the Śāntiparvan. In these texts, different authorities promote diverse teachings and definitions of Yoga. This diversity reflects the situation in ancient India, where different systems of Yoga co-existed. In the course of time, however, the Yogasūtra or Yogasūtras (YS), also known as Yogānuśāsanasūtra, has become the 'classical' text on Yoga and the basis for a system superseding other systems of Yoga. Although it has received an extraordinary amount of attention from modern scholars, as well as from contemporary Yoga practitioners, one should keep in mind that the system of the YS is but one Yoga system among others. The YS is strongly influenced by Sāṃkhya views. It consists of 194/195 aphorisms (*sūtra*), most likely of different origin and time periods, divided into four sections (*pāda*). Its compiler is unknown, but the text began to be ascribed to Patañjali probably around the tenth century CE. Because of its composite nature it is difficult to date the YS as a whole, and no scholarly consensus has been reached in this regard. Efforts to dissect the work into passages which could then be dated separately have not yielded conclusive results, the approaches differing considerably among scholars. The last redaction of the YS is likely to have been completed by the fourth century CE. The Yogasūtrabhāṣya from approximately the fifth/sixth century CE but attributed to the legendary (Veda-)Vyāsa or Bādarāyaṇa is the most influential commentary on the YS. The YS with the Yogasūtrabhāṣya is collectively called Pātañjalayogaśāstra. Modern authors often refer to the description of the Yoga with eight ancillary parts (*aṣṭāṅgayoga*)[3] found in YS 2.29 as 'the Yoga' taught in the YS and as *rājayoga*. However, the YS incorporates diverse teachings on Yoga, which were propagated by different groups, and of which *aṣṭāṅgayoga* is just one part. The word *rājayoga*, to be discussed in more detail in section 3, does not appear in the text at all.

Material on Yoga is scattered in different text genres, including passages in the Dharmaśāstra and Purāṇic literature, and in later Upaniṣads dealing specifically with Yoga and known as Yoga-Upaniṣads. The extant texts which are exclusively devoted to a tradition now often called *haṭhayoga* are compilations dating from a later period. Earlier material is included in Śaiva Tantras and in Tantric compendiums, but most of it is not easily accessible and therefore not widely known. The seventh-century work Tirumantiram by the Tamil poet Tirumūlar is an important early treatise on Yoga and a source for Śaiva Siddhānta philosophy. Sections of the Mālinīvijayottaratantra, an important Tantra in the tradition of the Trika school, present Śaiva Yoga teachings. They have recently been studied by Vasudeva (2004). Chapter 25 of Lakṣmaṇadeśika's tenth-/eleventh-century Śāradātilaka[4] should also be mentioned here. It gives a very concise summary of Yoga teachings in eighty-nine verses, and clearly presupposes a long development, drawing on different Yoga texts and traditions, from which it

---

[3] I translate Sanskrit *aṅga* as 'ancillary part' and not—as usual—'limb,' thereby modifying the translation of *aṅga* as 'ancillary/auxiliary' used by Vasudeva (see Vasudeva 2004: 367), who follows A. Sanderson.

[4] For a new edition and translation of this chapter, see Bühnemann 2000–2001, Volume II, section 2.6: Appendix 3 (= pp. 337–366).

presents teachings on the energy centres (*cakra*) in the human body and the *kuṇḍalinī* energy, among others.

The Yogaśāstra ascribed to Dattātreya[5] is written as a dialogue between Sāṃkṛti and Dattātreya. It seems to go also by the name Yogatattvaprakāśa and shares many passages with the Yogatattva-Upaniṣad, a later text included in the corpus of the Yoga-Upaniṣads.

Of great importance is the thirteenth-/fourteenth-century[6] Gorakṣaśataka (GŚ), one of several works ascribed to Gorakṣanātha/Gorakhnāth. This author, along with his teacher Matsyendranātha, is considered the founder of the movement of the Nātha-Yogins and of the system often called *haṭhayoga*. The GŚ, in spite of the component *śataka*, which refers to a collection of one hundred stanzas, is extant in several recensions with different verse numbers, ranging up to 200.

The Yogaśikhā-Upaniṣad[7] belongs to those Yoga-Upaniṣads which are likely to have either been expanded or composed in whole by an Advaitin in South India who borrowed passages from the Nātha texts.[8] The Upaniṣad shares many common passages with the Yogabīja attributed to Gorakṣanātha.[9]

The Śiva-Saṃhitā (ŚS) has been assigned to about the fifteenth century and shows the influence of Vedāntic thought.

The fifteenth-/sixteenth-century Haṭhapradīpikā[10] ('Small Lamp on Haṭha'; HP), also called Siddhāntamuktāvali[11] in the colophons of some manuscripts, is ascribed to Svātmārāma alias Ātmārāma. According to some manuscripts, the author belonged to the tradition of Sahajānanda. The commentary Yogaprakāśikā by Bālakṛṣṇa names Rāmanātha as the work's author. The text is extant in several recensions and preserved in many manuscripts, in which the number of verses varies, as does their

[5] In the introduction to his edition of the Haṭharatnāvalī, p. 34, Reddy speculates that the Yogaśāstra may have been written by an authority in the Dattātreya lineage. Bouy 1994: 118 dates the Yogaśāstra to as early as around 1300 CE.
[6] For a detailed discussion of the problem of the date and for different legends connected with Gorakṣanātha's life, see Nowotny 1976: 19ff. and Bouy 1994: 15–28.
[7] Bouy 1994: 31 dates this Upaniṣad to between 800 and 1300 CE.
[8] For more information, see Bouy 1994: 6.
[9] For a table showing common passages in both texts, see Bouy 1994: 104.
[10] In a note on their translation of HP2 1.1, Gharote/Devnath state that only the title Haṭhapradīpikā is attested in the manuscripts, not the widely-popularized name Haṭhayogapradīpikā. I therefore refer to the text as Haṭhapradīpikā.
[11] For a discussion of this title, see Gharote 1991: 247–248.

distribution in the chapters of the work. A new edition of the text in ten chapters (HP2) was recently published, but appears to contain material which was interpolated into the text later.[12] Of the extant commentaries on the text only three have so far been published, all of which belong to the nineteenth century CE and thus are several centuries later than the original text. The three published commentaries are the Haṭhapradīpikāvyākhyā Jyotsnā by Brahmānanda, who died in 1842 CE and wrote the commentary before 1830 CE,[13] the Haṭhapradīpikāvyākhyā Yogaprakāśikā by Bālakṛṣṇa from the first half of the nineteenth century CE and the Haṭhapradīpikāvṛtti by Bhojātmaja, written in 1852 CE in Marāṭhī.

The Haṭharatnāvalī (HR) by Śrīnivāsa from Āndhra,[14] South India, may tentatively be dated to between 1625 and 1695 CE.[15] The text is strongly influenced by the Haṭhapradīpikā, which it frequently quotes. The HR was commented on by Ambaragīra Yogin of unknown date and provenance.

The Gheraṇḍa-Saṃhitā (GS) was written by an author influenced by Vaiṣṇavism and Vedāntic thought. It is a compilation written in the form of a dialogue between Gheraṇḍa and his disciple Caṇḍakāpāli. The text has been assigned to the seventeenth/eighteenth century CE,[16] but this date is far from certain.

The Jogapradīpakā (JP)[17] was written by Jayatarāma, also known as Jaiyatarāma, Jayyatarāma, Jaitrāma or Jayatirāma in 1737.[18] The text was recently edited on the basis of two incomplete manuscripts (from Puṇe and Vārāṇasī). Its language can be characterized as a mixed Hindī, which contains Braj Bhāṣā, Kharī Bolī and semi-

---

[12] M.L. Gharote, however, considers this version to be the original text of the HP (Gharote 1991: 248). For a comparison of the versions extant in different manuscripts of the HP, see Gharote 1991. The first two chapters on *āsanas* and *prāṇāyāma* (with the Jyotsnā commentary) are currently being re-edited and translated by U. Bräutigam as part of a doctoral dissertation to be submitted to the University of Bonn, Germany.

[13] For these dates, see Gharote 1991b.

[14] According to the colophon of a manuscript (see HR1, introduction, p. 14 and p. 17, note 5, and HR2, p. 41, note 2), Śrīnivāsa belonged to the Tīrabhukta region, identified with Āndhra. See Reddy's discussion of this point in the introduction to HR1, pp. 14–15.

[15] See Reddy's discussion on the author's date in the introduction to his edition of the text (HR1, p. 10) and the introduction to the edition by Gharote/Devnath/Jha (HR2, p. xiv).

[16] For this time period, see the introduction to the edition of the GS, p. xxi.

[17] For more information on this text, see section 5.3.2. The text is also called Jogapradīpyakā, Jogapradīpā and Jogapradīpikā in some manuscripts.

Sanskritic forms.[19] Jayatarāma was a resident of Vṛndāvan and a disciple of Payaharibābā, also called Kṛṣṇadāsa, who occupied the seat of Galta (Jaipur). The JP is clearly influenced by Svātmārāma's Haṭhapradīpikā and acknowledges its debt to it.[20]

This brief survey of selected texts referred to in this book is by no means exhaustive but merely intended to provide the reader with some background for the following discussions. There exists a large body of literature on Yoga, both published and unpublished, and new texts continue to be edited from manuscripts.

[18] The correct date is *samvat* 1794, that is, 1737 CE. The introduction to the edition of the text, p. 1, converts *samvat* 1794 into 1718 CE, an error which Gharote corrected (email communication, May 8, 2002). Gode 1940: 312 assigns the text to the year 1729 CE.
[19] I am indebted to Dr. Charles Pain for this linguistic analysis.
[20] For such an acknowledgement, see, for example, the reference in verse 956 of the JP.

3. On the Terms *haṭhayoga* and *rājayoga*

It is now common in the secondary literature to refer to a tradition of Yoga which emphasizes physical practices such as postures and restraint of the breath as *haṭhayoga*. However, this term appears comparatively late in Sanskrit texts (although some of the practices subsumed under this term are of considerable age), and so does the distinction between *haṭhayoga* and *rājayoga* ('royal Yoga') in the way it is often made by modern authors. More research on the use of the terms *haṭhayoga* and *rājayoga* in texts of different time periods would be necessary to determine how they were understood by earlier authors. In a joint article, Kokaje/Gharote (1981) have made a beginning in this direction. In this section I will outline some of the shades of meaning of the terms in selected Sanskrit texts to demonstrate their different uses.

The word *haṭha* can mean 'force' in Sanskrit, and when combined with the word Yoga, *haṭhayoga* can be rendered as 'the applying of force' in a very general sense. In a technical sense, the term can be translated as 'the Yoga applying force.'[21] There are several interpretations of the term *haṭhayoga* that clearly differ from the understanding of many modern authors, who refer to the practice of postures as *haṭhayoga* and to practices described in the YS, especially the Yoga with eight ancillary parts (*aṣṭāṅgayoga*) in YS 2.29, as *rājayoga*.

It seems that at the time of Gorakṣanātha the word *haṭha* was understood as referring mainly to *prāṇāyāma* practice.[22] The terms *haṭhayoga* and *rājayoga* appear as parts of a fourfold Yoga in a number of later texts. According to texts such as Yogarāja-Upaniṣad 1cd-2ab, Yogatattva-Upaniṣad 19ff., Śiva-Saṃhitā 5.9, Yogaśikhā-Upaniṣad 1.129,[23] Śārṅgadharapaddhati, section 156, verse 1 (no. 4347) and Āgama-rahasya, *pūrvārdha* 27.4563, this fourfold Yoga consists of *mantrayoga*, *layayoga*, *haṭhayoga* and *rājayoga*. The Yogaśikhā-Upaniṣad and the Yogabīja state that these

[21] This interpretation of the term is supported by practices which aim at raising the *kuṇḍalinī* energy in the human body, making the *prāṇa* enter the *suṣumnā* channel and attempting to keep death away from the practitioner. The latter idea as a goal of Yoga is clearly expressed in HP 1.9cd, HP1 2.3cd (HP2 4.6cd) and HP1 2.40d (HP2 4.28d).

[22] For details on this point, see Kokaje/Gharote 1981: 198, 201.

[23] The passage is identical with Yogabīja 143cd–144.

four divisions form one comprehensive Yoga (*mahāyoga*). The four parts of this Yoga are interpreted differently in these texts.[24] From Yogabīja, verses 145–152 it appears that *haṭhayoga* is associated with *prāṇāyāma*, and *rājayoga* with *samādhi*. Yogabīja, verses 148cd–149ab, Yogaśikhā-Upaniṣad 1.133, Haṭharatnāvalī (HR2) 1.22 and several other texts divide the word *haṭha* into the components *ha* and *ṭha*, signifying the sun (*ha*) and moon (*ṭha*), and thereby support the link to *prāṇāyāma* practice. Yogamārgaprakāśikā 137[25] takes the syllable *ha* to designate Śaṃkara/Śiva and *ṭha* to mean Śakti.[26]

The fourfold *mahāyoga* is also described in Haṭharatnāvalī 1.7cd–23. In that text *rājayoga* is understood as a mental state, and *haṭhayoga* as a practice leading to that state. The system of *haṭhayoga* is defined as including ten *mudrā*s, eight *kriyā*s, eight *kumbhaka*s and eighty-four *āsana*s (HR2 1.17). Both *haṭhayoga* and *rājayoga* are said to be dependent on one another (HR2, 1.18).

Aparokṣānubhūti (verses 143–144), a work attributed to Śaṃkara,[27] may be among the earlier texts to use the two terms *rājayoga* and *haṭhayoga*. Verses 102–103 describe a Yoga with fifteen ancillary parts (*aṅga*), which are enumerated in section 4.2 below. These ancillary parts are explained one after the other in subsequent sections of the text and include *āsana*, *mūlabandha* and *prāṇasaṃyamana* among others, which are interpreted in specific ways in keeping with Vedāntic thought. Verses 143–144 of the text then call the Yoga with fifteen ancillary parts *rājayoga* and recommend it to a practitioner whose mind is purified. For the less advanced practitioner this system of *rājayoga* is recommended in combination with *haṭhayoga*, a term that remains

[24] See, for example, Yogatattva-Upaniṣad, 21ff. and the passage Yogaśikhā-Upaniṣad 1.130–136ab; the latter passage is identical with Yogabīja, 145–152.

[25] The text is quoted in Kokaje/Gharote 1981: 201.

[26] This interpretation of the two syllables of the word *haṭha* echoes the established interpretation of the two syllables *haṃ* and *saḥ*, which constitute the 'non-recitation' (*ajapā*) *gāyatrī* or *haṃsaḥ* mantra, in which *haṃ* (or sometimes *ha*) is said to be the sound of exhalation, and *saḥ* (or *sa*), the sound of inhalation. (For an attempt to explain how the syllables *ha* and *ṭha* [the latter syllable replacing *sa*] came to signify the sun and moon, see Dave/Bhole 1987.) The syllables *ha* and *sa*, too, are said to represent the sun and the moon or Śiva and Śakti respectively.

[27] We do not have exact information on the date of composition or compilation of the Aparokṣānubhūti. Bouy 1994: 62 dates the text to between the eighth and thirteenth centuries. A large section of the Aparokṣānubhūti, including the description of the Yoga with fifteen ancillary parts (but not the verses distinguishing between *rājayoga* and *haṭhayoga*), also forms part of the Tejobindu-Upaniṣad.

unexplained in the text.

Verses 143–144 of the Aparokṣānubhūti have been commented on by fourteenth-century Vidyāraṇya-Mādhava in his Dīpikā. It is significant that this commentator explains the term *haṭhayoga* as 'the well-known Yoga with eight ancillary parts described by Patañjali,' and understands *rājayoga* as the Vedāntic Yoga with fifteen ancillary parts. In his Jīvanmuktiviveka Vidyāraṇya-Mādhava does not use the term *rājayoga* at all. The few occurrences of the word *haṭhayoga* support an interpretation in a more general sense of a 'forceful method' (employed by Yogins) as contrasted with a 'gentle method' (*mṛduyoga*).[28]

Like Vidyāraṇya-Mādhava, the anonymous author of the preface to a nineteenth-century Gujarati work Āgamaprakāśa[29] regards *haṭhayoga* as Patañjali's Yoga system. However, he deviates from Vidyāraṇya-Mādhava when he explains *rājayoga* (spelt 'rājyayoga') as the Yoga of the Kaulas.

The sixteenth-century author Vijñānabhikṣu, finally, presents the more familiar distinction between *rājayoga* and *haṭhayoga*. For this author, *rājayoga* is concerned with mental processes, and *haṭhayoga* with posture (*āsana*), restraint of the breath (*prāṇāyāma*) and the purification of the channels (*nāḍī*).[30]

There is a reference to two traditions of *haṭha* in the fourteenth-century compilation Śārṅgadharapaddhati by Śārṅgadhara, sections 157–158. They are specified as

1) the tradition of Gorakṣa and his followers and
2) the tradition of Mṛkaṇḍaputra/Mārkaṇḍeya and his followers.

A similar passage appears in the compilation Āgamarahasya, *pūrvārdha* 27.4677ff., but in that text the first tradition of Yoga is associated with Gorakṣanātha's teacher Matsyendranātha. According to tradition, Matsyendranātha was the first teacher of *haṭhayoga* after Ādinātha (Śiva). While Gorakṣanātha and/or Matsyendranātha are thus considered to be the founders of *haṭhayoga* and are included in the group of the Nine Nāthas and in Siddha lineages, the identity of Mārkaṇḍeya remains unclear.

---

[28] See Jīvanmuktiviveka (edited by Sastri/Ayyangar), p. 14, 13–14, p. 14, 18 and p. 88, 8.
[29] For this work and a translation of its preface into English, see Rinehard/Stewart 2000: 276.
[30] For this distinction, see Vijñānabhikṣu's Yogasārasaṃgraha, p. 39, 5–6 (Sanskrit text) and p. 55 (translation) and Vijñānabhikṣu's Sāṃkhyasāra, *uttarabhāga*, 6.3.

Section 156, verse 18 (no. 4364) of the Śārṅgadharapaddhati[31] speaks of the *rājayoga* as practised by Dattātreya and his followers. The name of Dattātreya as a teacher of Yoga is associated with a section in the Mārkaṇḍeya-Purāṇa, which also speaks about posture and the restraint of the breath,[32] and with a text titled Yogaśāstra (see section 2 of this book), among others.

The Gheraṇḍa-Saṃhitā does not use the term *haṭhayoga* at all. The text refers to its Yoga, which consists of *āsanas*, *prāṇāyāma*, etc. as *ghaṭa(stha)yoga*, the 'Yoga (pertaining to) the body (*ghaṭa*).' [33] It is tempting to suggest a connection between the words *haṭha* and *ghaṭa*.[34] However, the etymology of the term *haṭha* has not been explained convincingly,[35] and the word *ghaṭa* cannot easily be derived from it.[36]

Yogaśikhā-Upaniṣad 1.136cd–138 offers a different explanation of the word *rājayoga* by interpreting the term as the union of menstrual blood (*rajas*) and semen (*retas*). Similarly, Yogabīja (verse 89) gives the union of *rajas* and *retas* as one of the meanings of the term Yoga. Although the eighteenth-century commentator on the Upaniṣad named Upaniṣadbrahmayogin glosses the union of *rajas* and *retas* in more general terms as the union of Śakti and Śiva, it is clear that the Upaniṣad's explanation of the word *rājayoga* as well as the Yogabīja's explanation of Yoga take Tantric practices into account in which these two substances were mingled and used in ritual. The anonymous author of the preface to the above-mentioned Āgamaprakāśa must also have had such practices in mind when he explained *rājayoga* as the Yoga of the Kaulas. Based on the Yogaśikhā-Upaniṣad's explanation, D.G. White suggests a new interpretation of the term *rājayoga* as the 'consumption of male and female sexual emissions.'[37]

---

[31] This section of the text is also found in Āgamarahasya, *pūrvārdha* 27.4669.
[32] For this section of the text, see Pargiter's translation of the Purāṇa, pp. 193–207.
[33] For the term *ghaṭa(stha)yoga*, see GS 1.2 and the colophons to several chapters of the text.
[34] In his notes on GS 1.1, P. Thomi (Gheraṇḍasaṃhitā: Sanskrit-deutsch. Wichtrach: Institut für Indologie, 1993) suggested just such a derivation of the word *haṭha* from *ghaṭa* (*ghaṭa* > *haṭa* > *haṭha*).
[35] According to Mayrhofer, the etymology of neither *haṭha* nor the word *ghaṭa* has been explained convincingly (Mayrhofer 1986–2001, volume 3: 530–531, s.v. *haṭha*; Mayrhofer 1986–2001, volume 3: 167, s.v. *ghaṭa*).
[36] H.H. Hock (email communication, December 5, 2002) explains that it would be difficult to combine the two forms *haṭha* and *ghaṭa* on linguistic grounds.
[37] See White 2003: 81–82 and 295, note 86 for this interpretation. The reference from the Amanaskayoga, which he cites (White 2003: 81 and 295, note 86) to strengthen his argument,

In the West, the term *rājayoga* has been popularized by Swami Vivekananda (1863–1902) through his influential treatise "Rājayoga," written in 1896. In that work he uses the term to refer to Patañjali's Yoga with eight ancillary parts.[38] However, the term *rājayoga* does not appear in the YS at all, and references to *rājayoga* as a system of Yoga are few in the literature. In many texts *rājayoga* does not refer to a system of Yoga but to a mental state and is used synonymously with the word *samādhi*.[39] The fact that texts such as Haṭhapradīpikā 1.1 explain *haṭhayoga* as the stairway to *rājayoga* (that is, to *samādhi*) seems to have contributed to the confusion.

In the course of time many later authorities have attempted to combine the Yoga with eight ancillary parts (*aṣṭāṅgayoga*) taught in YS 2.29 with techniques of the so-called *haṭhayoga*. Thus Yogatattva-Upaniṣad 24–27 combines the eight ancillary parts of YS 2.29 with twelve other practices including 'seals' (*mudrā*) and 'energy locks' (*bandha*), and defines this Yoga as *haṭhayoga*. However, the approach to Yoga in the YS, which is influenced by Sāṃkhya thought and emphasizes mental processes, and the approach to Yoga taken by the Nāthas as laid down in later *haṭhayoga* texts clearly differ. In the YS there is no mention of *bandhas*, *mudrās*, *cakras* or *kuṇḍalinī*, practices and concepts which take on great importance in the Yoga of the Nāthas. The teachings collected in the YS originated in a different milieu and breathe a different spirit than those advocated by proponents of the Nātha tradition, which employ physical and physiological means. Although the goal of *haṭhayoga* is also defined as

---

does not support his interpretation. Amanaskayoga 2.33–37 criticizes different practices of ascetics, including *vajrolī*, and makes it clear that only the practitioner of *rājayoga* attains success. Amanaskayoga 2.3–6ab describes this *rājayoga*, which is said to be a combination of external and internal *mudrās* (the *śāmbhavī mudrā* is extolled in 3.20 and passim) and superior to all Yogas. Two explanation of the meaning of *rājayoga* are given. The first (2.4) derives *rājayoga* from the word *rājatva* ('sovereignty'), and the second from the verbal root *rāj* ('to shine'). This *rājayoga* is held to be the Amanaskayoga advocated by the text.

[38] See Vivekananda (1896) 1978: xi: "The subject of the present book is that form of Yoga known as Raja-Yoga. The aphorisms of Patanjali are the highest authority on Raja-Yoga, and form its text book." For a detailed discussion of Vivekananda's work "Rājayoga," see Michelis 2004: 149–180.

[39] HP1 4.3–4 asserts that the following terms are synonyms: *rājayoga*, *samādhi*, *unmanī* and *manonmanī*; further, immortality (*amaratva*), merging (*laya*), truth (*tattva*), empty and not empty (*śūnyāśūnya*), the supreme state (*paramapada*), transcending the mind (*amanaska*), non-duality (*advaita*), without support (*nirālamba*), unstained (*nirañjana*), liberation while alive (*jīvanmukti*), the natural (*sahajā*) state and the fourth (*turyā*) (state). The corresponding stanzas HP2 8.50–51 offer a number of variant readings. GS 7.17 also asserts that *rājayoga*, *samādhi*, *unmanī* and the natural state (*sahajāvasthā*) are synonyms.

liberation, the Nāthas' understanding of what liberation means, namely escape from death and immortality, differs. The occurrences of the terms *rājayoga* and *haṭhayoga* to distinguish these two different approaches to Yoga are limited in texts and not based on a traditional use of the terms.

4. The Place and Function of Āsanas in Yoga Systems

4.1 The Term Āsana

The word *āsana* can be translated as 1) sitting, abiding, 2) a seat or throne, 3) a sitting position or posture, among other possible meanings. In Yoga, *āsana* is a technical term for posture, for which synonyms such as *pīṭha* or *niṣadana* are also used.[40] Some texts offer specialized philosophic interpretations of the term, such as the aforementioned Vedānta text Aparokṣānubhūti (verse 112), which defines *āsana* as 'that in which continuous reflection on *brahman* is easily possible.' Another unidentified text defines *āsana* as 'the establishment in the original state.'[41] Āsana is also a term for positions in archery and wrestling.[42]

4.2 Āsana as an Ancillary Part (*aṅga*) of Yoga Systems

Posture is counted as an ancillary part (*aṅga*) of many Yoga systems, and is defined and described as such in many texts. However, the place of *āsana*s within the systems varies, and so does the importance attached to them. In some Yoga systems, such as the Śaiva systems of Yoga with their six ancillary parts (Vasudeva 2004: 397–398), *āsana* is not listed separately as an ancillary part, but nevertheless some seated postures suitable for meditation are described. In this section I will briefly survey the place of *āsana*s in different Yoga systems, thereby taking note of divisions according to the number of the ancillary parts (*aṅga*). I will merely refer to selected texts and caution the reader that although the same or similar terms are used in them, the specific definitions of the ancillary parts often vary between systems, as do the practices subsumed under these terms. Such variations in the interpretation of the terms will not

---

[40] The word *pīṭha* is used in HP1 1.39 and HP2 2.25; for *niṣadana*, see the commentary attributed to Vyāsa on YS 2.46. Another, but less common, synonym is *pṛthvī*, which literally means 'the earth.' In his commentary Jyotsnā on HP 3.126 (HP2 7.10) Brahmānanda glosses the word *pṛthvī* as *āsana*.

[41] This definition is quoted by Gharote 1999: 16, 23 from an unidentified text.

[42] For this use of the term *āsana*, see Sjoman 1999: 45.

be apparent from a mere listing of the ancillary parts of different Yoga systems.

Yoga systems with eight or six ancillary parts are the ones most commonly found in texts. In many systems with eight ancillary parts (*aṣṭāṅga*), *āsana* is the third ancillary part, following the great rules (*yama*) and minor rules (*niyama*). The standard list in YS 2.29 consists of the 1) great rules (*yama*), 2) minor rules (*niyama*), 3) posture (*āsana*), 4) restraint of the breath (*prāṇāyāma*), 5) withdrawal of sense organs (from sense objects) (*pratyāhāra*), 6) fixation (of the mind on a certain object) (*dhāraṇā*), 7) meditation (*dhyāna*) and 8) absorption (*samādhi*).

Yoga systems with six ancillary parts[43] usually do not include the great and minor rules. However, one should not conclude that these systems did not emphasize or value the rules. In Tantric texts, the rules are often articulated in other sections of the same work. The texts propagating a Yoga with six ancillary parts have broadly been divided into two groups.[44] Only one of the two groups of texts includes *āsana*. Thus, for example, *āsana* is entirely lacking in a later and most likely interpolated[45] passage, Maitrāyaṇīya-Upaniṣad 6.18, which lists the six ancillary parts as: 1) restraint of the breath (*prāṇāyāma*), 2) withdrawal of sense organs (*pratyāhāra*), 3) meditation (*dhyāna*), 4) fixation (*dhāraṇā*), 5) discernment (*tarka*) between what should be cultivated and what should be rejected and 6) absorption (*samādhi*). But *āsana* is included, for example, in the second verse of the Yogacūḍāmaṇi-Upaniṣad, where we find: 1) posture (*āsana*), 2) restraint of the breath (*prāṇasaṃrodha*), 3) withdrawal of

[43] A Yoga with six ancillary parts is found in a number of sources, including a few Dharmaśāstra texts, Purāṇas and some of the Yoga-Upaniṣads. In texts of the Āgamic/Tantric tradition (Brunner 1994: 439–440 and Rastogi 1992: 247ff.) this Yoga is more common than the Yoga with eight ancillary parts. A considerable amount of research has been done on *ṣaḍaṅgayoga* in Buddhist and Hindu texts; see, for example, Grönbold 1969: 134–147 and 1996. Recently Vasudeva 2004 studied the *ṣaḍaṅgayoga* in the Mālinīvijayottaratantra of the Trika. For a useful survey of *ṣaḍaṅgayoga* in different varieties of Śaiva Yoga, see Vasudeva 2004: 367–436. A survey of recent scholarship on the topic is found in Sferra 2000: 11–37.

[44] Grönbold 1983 divides the texts describing *ṣaḍaṅgayoga* into two groups: 1) those which include *āsana* and 2) those which include *tarka*, that is, discernment between what should be cultivated and what should be rejected. The second group is again subdivided into two groups. In Grönbold's opinion, the first group represents a spurious *ṣaḍaṅgayoga*, since it simply omits the first two ancillary parts (that is, the great and minor rules) of the *aṣṭāṅgayoga* (Grönbold 1983: 184). However, as Vasudeva 2004: 370 observes, the differences between individual Yoga systems may be greater than they may appear to be at first sight despite the similarities of terms. One major difference is that unlike Patañjali's Yoga, the Śaiva systems of Yoga are strictly theistic.

sense organs (*pratyāhāra*), 4) fixation (*dhāraṇā*), 5) meditation (*dhyāna*) and 6) absorption (*samādhi*).[46]

A Yoga with four ancillary parts which includes posture appears in several texts. A verse from the unedited work Videhamuktikathana,[47] also found in Yogarāja-Upaniṣad, verse 2 and quoted in Śārṅgadharapaddhati, section 156, verse 2 (no. 4348), enumerates the four as 1) posture (*āsana*), 2) restraint of the breath (*prāṇasaṃrodha*), 3) meditation (*dhyāna*) and absorption (*samādhi*). HP1 1.56 (see HP2 3.3) teaches a different Yoga with four ancillary parts, consisting of 1) posture (*āsana*), 2) retention of breath (*kumbhaka* = *prāṇāyāma*), 3) techniques called 'seal' (*mudrā*) and 4) concentration on the inner sound (*nādānusandhāna*) leading to *samādhi*. But another passage in one recension of this text (HP2 1.35; see GŚ 4) also refers to a Yoga with six ancillary parts.

Āsana is lacking in the five-fold Yoga explained in Vāyu-Purāṇa 10.76[48] and ascribed to Maheśvara/Śiva. This Yoga consists of 1) restraint of the breath (*prāṇāyāma*), 2) meditation (*dhyāna*), 3) withdrawal of sense organs (*pratyāhāra*), 4) fixation (*dhāraṇā*) and 5) recollection (*smaraṇa*).

Gheraṇḍa-Saṃhitā 1.10–11 teaches a Yoga with seven ancillary parts, in which *āsana* functions as the second ancillary part. The seven parts are 1) the six purification practices (*ṣaṭkarman*), 2) posture (*āsana*), 3) techniques called 'seal' (*mudrā*), 4) withdrawal of sense organs (*pratyāhāra*), 5) restraint of the breath (*prāṇāyāma*), 6) meditation (*dhyāna*) and 7) absorption (*samādhi*).

A section (verses 102ff.) in the aforementioned Aparokṣānubhūti, which is also found in the Tejobindu-Upaniṣad (1.15ff.), teaches a Yoga with fifteen ancillary parts (*pañcadaśāṅga*), in which *āsana* occupies the seventh position. The fifteen ancillary parts are 1) great rules (*yama*), 2) minor rules (*niyama*), 3) renunciation (*tyāga*), 4) silence (*mauna*), 5) location (*deśa*), 6) time (*kāla*), 7) posture (*āsana*), 8) root lock

---

[45] The Maitrāyaṇīya-Upaniṣad, which J.A.B. van Buitenen studied in detail, has undergone several redactions. The passage 6.18 was certainly not part of the first redaction of the text.

[46] The same verse appears in a number of other texts, including Dhyānabindu-Upaniṣad 41 and the fourteenth-century compilation Śārṅgadharapaddhati by Śārṅgadhara, section 157, verse 3 (no. 4374) (see Grönbold 1983: 184). It also appears with variants in GŚ 4 and other Yoga texts of the Gorakṣa school.

[47] For this work, see Grönbold 1969: 144–145 and 1983: 182.

[48] The text identifies this Yoga as Pāśupatayoga.

(*mūlabandha*), 9) equilibrium of the body (*dehasāmya*), 10) fixed vision (*dṛksthiti*), 11) restraint of the breath (*prāṇasaṃyamana*), 12) withdrawal of senses (*pratyāhāra*), 13) fixation (*dhāraṇā*), 14) meditation on the self (*ātmadhyāna*) and 15) absorption (*samādhi*). At first sight the fifteen ancillary parts appear to be an expanded version of the Yoga system with eight ancillary parts as found in the YS,[49] but a closer examination of the text shows that each term is interpreted according to non-dualist Vedāntic thought and is given an entirely new meaning, with emphasis on the practitioner's mental condition. Posture (*āsana*) is defined as 'that in which continuous reflection on *brahman* is easily possible' (verse 112) and is distinguished from a posture which causes discomfort. The next verse then singles out Siddhāsana, the name of a traditional Yogic posture, and offers a Vedāntic reinterpretation of it.

4.3 The Function of Āsanas in Yoga Systems

YS 2.46 recommends any seated posture or form of sitting (*āsana*) which is firm and comfortable for the practice of the restraint of the breath (*prāṇāyāma*) and the other ancillary parts. The fifth-/sixth-century commentary on the YS attributed to Vyāsa specifies eleven *āsana*s and indicates by an 'etc.' that the author knew additional postures. These postures are meditative *āsana*s, which enable the practitioner to sit with his chest, neck and head held erect. Similarly, many other Yoga texts recommend a small number of meditative postures, which the practitioner can hold comfortably for a prolonged period of time. In his commentary (Bhāṣya) on Brahmasūtras 4.1.7(–10), the philosopher Śaṃkara, who flourished between 650 and 800 CE, elaborates on the Sūtra's statement that meditation should be done in a seated position. He makes a case for seated postures such as the lotus posture, explaining that meditation, which is defined as a flow of identical thoughts, cannot be practised while walking or running because movement distracts the mind. Even when standing the mind is occupied with holding the body and unable to examine subtle matters. When lying down one may suddenly fall asleep. Other texts expand the number of postures by adding *āsana*s for strength, health and suppleness of body. Thus HP1 1.17 states that *āsana*s bring about firmness, health and lightness of body. All traditional systems of Yoga, however,

[49] For this observation, see also Grönbold 1983: 183.

assign a preparatory and subordinate place to *āsanas* in the pursuit of liberation from the cycle of rebirth. Neither the YS nor the Upaniṣads nor the epic texts on Yoga emphasize *āsanas*. Even most texts of the Nātha or *haṭha* traditions teach a very limited number of *āsanas*, and these are often combined with 'energy locks' (*bandha*), that is, muscular contractions and other practices, such as *prāṇāyāma*. This view of the subordinate position of *āsanas* clearly differs from that of most modern Yoga schools.

HP1 1.18 (HP2 2.4) divides *āsanas* according to two traditions:
1) *āsanas* in the tradition of sages (*muni*) such as Vasiṣṭha and
2) *āsanas* as taught by Yogins such as Matsyendra(nātha).

This division may be suggestive of a tradition of meditative postures and another tradition of postures taught by physical culturists, such as the Nāthas. The identity of Vasiṣṭha remains unclear. Vasiṣṭha is a name appearing in many lineages of teachers or sages. His name is associated with the Yogakāṇḍa of the Vasiṣṭha-Saṃhitā, which is sometimes called Yogayājñavalkya[saṃhitā] and perhaps dates from about 1250 CE. Matsyendranātha is traditionally considered the founder of *haṭhayoga* and would naturally be associated with *āsanas*. He features prominently in the group of the Nine Nāthas and in some Siddha lineages.

We know little about the development of *āsana* traditions over time. While the texts of the Nātha/*haṭha* tradition teach relatively few postures, the number of postures gradually expanded within circles of practitioners who wanted to derive physical benefits from them. Thus the postures were isolated from the general framework of Yoga and combined with physical exercises. In modern India, *āsanas* have also been incorporated into athletic routines, including those of wrestlers (*malla*). The practice of performing *āsanas* on the wrestler's post (*mallakhāmba*)[50] and on a rope (*rajju*) continues in Mahārāṣṭra. Here the function of *āsanas* is to make the body supple and strong. Health and physical development were also the goal of modern proponents of Yoga such as Swami Kuvalayananda (1883–1966) from Kaivalyadhama near Puṇe in Mahārāṣṭra, who was instrumental in introducing *āsanas* into the curricula of Indian

[50] Yogic *āsanas* only figure among other types of exercises and movements performed on the wrestler's post. For a description of *āsanas* performed on the wrestler's post, see Mujumdar 1950: 359–363. According to Gharote 1989: 42, *āsanas* on a rope are described in the text Kapālakuraṇṭaka, also known as Haṭhābhyāsapaddhati. In the notes to his edition of the HR

schools. Health benefits are likewise the goal of most modern Yoga schools in India and abroad, which teach many postures and few or no breathing techniques, and exclude the practices considered most important in *haṭhayoga*, which aim at raising the *kuṇḍalinī*. A relatively new development in India and abroad is the performance of *āsana*s in Yoga contests as part of competitive sport. This is referred to as Yoga Sports and includes such subdisciplines as Athletic Yoga, Olympic Yoga Sport and Artistic Yoga Sport.

The *āsana* practice of the many modern Yoga schools in India and the West is not directly based on or otherwise connected with any known textual tradition. Even so, modern Yoga schools regularly invoke the authority of the YS despite the fact that there is little in their curricula that bears resemblance to the teachings in that text. One reason for this is that the YS is the best-known text on Yoga in the West and believed to be of great antiquity. It is accessible in a number of translations. Claiming the authority of such a text adds to the prestige of one's school and the authenticity of its teachings. Some exponents of modern Yoga have also attempted to draw a more specific connection between their *āsana* practice and the ancillary parts of Patañjali's Yoga as taught in YS 2.29. To defend themselves against criticism from traditionalists, who accuse modern Yoga teachers of being unfaithful to traditional Yoga by promoting postures instead of cultivating spiritual practices, several contemporary teachers have begun to claim that all ancillary parts of Patañjali's eightfold Yoga are inherent in their *āsana* practice. They assert that the ancillary parts either unfold naturally *after* or are even experienced *during* the practice of the postures. These teachers include proponents of the Aṣṭāṅgayoga of Pattabhi Jois,[51] of Iyengar Yoga[52]

(p. 139), Reddy dates the Kapālakuraṇṭaka to later than the seventeenth-century HR. For the use of *āsanas* by traditional wrestlers as gleaned from the Malla-Purāṇa, see Gharote 1998.

[51] See A. Grover Pace's article "Ashtanga Yoga in the Tradition of Sri K. Pattabhi Jois" on the official website of the Aṣṭāṅgayoga Research Institute in Mysore (retrieved December 1, 2002 from http://www.ashtanga.com/html/AYarticle.html). Āsanas are advocated as the foundation for the restraint of the breath (*prāṇāyāma*) and as the key to the development of the great and minor rules (*yama/niyama*). When these four ancillary parts have been developed, the others "will spontaneously evolve over time."

[52] See K. Baier's article "Iyengar and The Yoga Tradition" (retrieved December 1, 2002 from http://www.iyengar-yoga.com/articles/yogatradition/) on the official website of the Iyengar Yoga Institute in Puṇe. Baier suggests that B.K.S. Iyengar affirms the simultaneous presence of all the ancillary parts of Yoga in the *āsana* practice and not a gradual development of these

and B.K.S. Iyengar[53] himself, all of whom offer slightly different but similar views on the issue.[54] In the following statement Yogi Amrit Desai (b. 1932), founder of Kripalu Yoga, claims experiences which indicate the presence of all ancillary parts of the eightfold Yoga in the performance of *āsanas*:

> In my posture flow experiences I was spontaneously and naturally entering into all the stages of Ashtang yoga simultaneously: asanas (postures), pranayama (specific breathing patterns), pratyahara (internalization of the outgoing attention), dharana (concentration), dhyana (deep meditation), and ultimately samadhi (complete union with universal consciousness ...). These stages are usually practiced in a linear, willful fashion, but in my case they unfolded one from the other in a natural, organic fashion, with each succeeding stage adding itself to the others, until all were experienced simultaneously in a peak yogic experience of self-transcendence. In this final stage of samadhi, movement sometimes continues, or the body may subside into complete stillness.[55]

Be this as it may, a study of the classical texts shows that modern Yoga teachers' interpretation of Yoga as the exclusive practice of different postures is not supported by the authority of the ancient texts on Yoga, nor is it in line with the view of *āsanas* as a preliminary foundation of practice in traditional Yoga texts.

We do not have access to source materials that would enable us to trace the history of modern developments in *āsana* practice. It is possible that some important texts on Yoga that may provide some clues about historical developments have not yet come to light or have been lost. In any case, one needs to recall that Yoga practices were traditionally carried out individually under the supervision and guidance of a teacher. These teachers were bearers of oral traditions which are difficult to trace. The

---

ancillary parts on the basis of the postures. This view apparently reflects a position which Iyengar has adopted more recently.

53 See the following statement in Iyengar 1989: 50: "All the eight limbs of yoga have their place within the practice of āsana." Iyengar 1989: 50ff. proceeds to interpret the great and minor rules (*yama/niyama*) as principles to be observed in the practice of *āsanas*.

54 Some teachers of Kaivalyadhama (Bhole/Jha/Sahay 1979) also argue for a greater appreciation of *āsanas* as a means of attaining meditative states. They cite YS 2.47 in support of their view, a *sūtra* which refers to *āsanas* as a preparation to meditating on the infinite (*anantasamāpatti*). However, they do not go to the extreme of asserting that all eight ancillary parts of Yoga can be experienced by just practising *āsanas*.

55 The quotation is taken from Desai 1985: I-4. According to Desai 1985: I-30, five ancillary parts of Patañjali's Yoga (*āsana, prāṇāyāma, pratyāhāra, dhāraṇā* and *dhyāna*) are practised in Kripalu Yoga. The great and minor rules (*yama/niyama*) are not considered part of formal practice but rather to be the foundation. The last ancillary part, absorption (*samādhi*), emerges naturally and can therefore not be included in formal practice either.

personal accounts of the American Theos Bernard (1908–1947), who underwent a traditional course of Yoga near Ranchi in North India in the 1930s, show that at that time Yoga practices similar to those recorded in texts such as the Haṭhapradīpikā were still observed and orally transmitted.

Sjoman's research on the origins of modern *āsana* traditions identified a section describing a wide range of postures in one extant version of the Śrītattvanidhi as an important link between the ancient and modern traditions. In his study Sjoman is mainly concerned with the Yoga tradition of the Mysore Palace, from which T. Krishnamacharya (Krishnamacariar) (1888–1989) and his two students B.K.S. Iyengar (b. 1918) and K. Pattabhi Jois (b. 1915) emerged, both of whom developed their own distinct styles of practice. In identifying factors that contributed to the development of the Mysore Yoga tradition, Sjoman 1999: 44 stresses the influence of the exercise arenas (*vyāyāmaśāla*) run by ascetic orders and wrestlers. He concludes that the Yoga system of the Mysore Palace as known to Krishnamacharya was a syncretistic system drawing heavily on a gymnastic text, the Vyāyāmadīpikā, and that it incorporated influences from the wrestlers' tradition, indigenous exercises and even Western gymnastics.[56] Other Yoga traditions have not been examined in such detail, leaving much scope for future research.

[56] For more information, see the discussion in Sjoman 1999: 55–60.

5. Eighty-four Āsanas in Yoga

5.1 The Number of Āsanas in Yoga Systems

The number of *āsanas* mentioned in Yoga texts varies greatly. Tirumūlar's Tirumantiram, section 3, for example, lists the following eight postures from an alleged 180 postures: Bhadrāsana, Gomukhāsana, Padmāsana, Siṃhāsana, Sthirāsana, Vīrāsana, Sukhāsana and Svastikāsana. Some postures referred to in Śaiva Tantras are listed in Vasudeva 2004: 397–401. Gorakṣaśataka 5ab states that there are as many *āsanas* as species of living beings. Several texts claim that eighty-four *āsanas* were taught by Śiva from a total of eighty-four *lakṣas*, that is, eighty-four times one hundred thousand (8,400,000) *āsanas*. The Gorakṣaśataka may be the oldest of these sources. Similar statements are found in later *haṭhayoga* texts, such as HP1 1.33 (HP2 2.3), ŚS 3.84 and GS 2.1-2. However, the texts then proceed to describe a much smaller number of *āsanas* as important, which are said to have been selected from the eighty-four. The number and names of the *āsanas* chosen differ in the texts. From the legendary eighty-four *āsanas*, GŚ 7 selects only two *āsanas* as important: Siddhāsana and the lotus posture (Kamalāsana). HP1 1.34[57] and ŚS 3.84 name only four postures. In the case of the Haṭhapradīpikā, these are Siddhāsana, the lotus posture (Padmāsana), Siṃhāsana and Bhadrāsana, among which Siddhāsana is considered the best. The Śiva-Saṃhitā specifies the four postures as Siddhāsana, Padmāsana, Ugrāsana (also called Paś-cimottāna) and Svastikāsana. Gheraṇḍa-Saṃhitā 2.2 teaches as many as thirty-two postures. The Yogaśāstra of Dattātreya, verses 66–67, also refers to 8,400,000 *āsanas*, of which the lotus posture is considered the most important. This posture is indeed of great importance since it is mentioned in ancient texts and also plays an important role in Indian iconography. The actual number of postures described in other later Yoga

---

[57] In my opinion, HP2 represents an inflated version of the text, in that it contains interpolated material. The section HP2 2.5–18, which is obviously an interpolated passage, describes eleven *āsanas*, while 2.19 states that only four *āsanas* have been selected from a total of eighty-four. These four postures are described in 2.21–38. There are considerable differences among the versions found in manuscripts of the HP. Gharote 1991: 244–246 describes a manuscript of the HP from Jodhpur which lists as many as one hundred *āsanas*.

texts occasionally attains the sacred number 108.[58] The Yoga section preserved in one of two versions of the Śrītattvanidhi, which was studied by Sjoman 1999, teaches as many as 122 *āsanas*. The number of *āsana*s in contemporary traditions also varies. While most traditions teach a smaller number of postures that can be learnt by the average practitioner with some amount of practice, there is also a noticeable tendency to expand the number of *āsana*s by introducing new variants. Dhirendra Brahmachari 1970 describes 108 postures plus the Sun Salutation; Iyengar 1984: 507–512, about 200 *āsanas*; and Yogeshwaranand Parmahansa 1987, as many as 300. The recent publication Mittra 2003 is a collection of photographs of 608 postures, which were selected from a "Master Yoga Chart" featuring 908 postures, which Mittra published earlier. While some of the postures were developed by Mittra himself, most were collected from books and from information provided by students of different traditions.

5.2 The Number Eighty-four

The number eighty-four continues to hold special symbolic significance for authors of ancient and modern Yoga texts, who honour this number in their *āsana* systems.[59] One encounters the number in other contexts as well. Thus, we find various lists of names of eighty-four Mahāsiddhas, a description of eighty-four phallic representations (*liṅga*) of Śiva,[60] listings of names of eighty-four Tantras and so forth.[61] Eighty-four postures

---

[58] For 108 *āsana*s in the Yogāsanamālā and the Jodhpur manuscript of the Haṭhapradīpikā, see Gharote 1999: 25.

[59] Hirschi 1997 honours the number eighty-four in a set of posture cards. As Hirschi 1997: 5 explains: "I've adhered to the body postures of classic yoga in the selection of exercises. Even the *Hatha Yoga Pradipika*, one of the oldest yoga writings, speaks of eighty-four positions. However, very few of these are actually described, and by no means can all these exercises be done, unless you've been doing yoga since you were a small child. This set also consists of eighty-four cards...." Other modern compilers of lists of eighty-four *āsana*s include Venkateshananda (†)/Metcalfe/Roy 1984, V. Bretz (Sukadev) of Yoga-Vidya, Germany (retrieved December 10, 2002 from http://www.yoga-vidya.de/Asana_Uebungsplaene/ Fortg-Flex.html) and L. Spaulding of Yoga East, Inc., Louisville, Kentucky, who compiled an (unpublished) list of eighty-four postures for her teachers' training.

[60] This description is found in the section titled *caturaśītiliṅgamāhātmya* of the Āvantya-khaṇḍa of the Skanda-Purāṇa.

[61] For some information on eighty-four as a mystical number classifying different entities, see Dasgupta 1976: 204. An extensive list of texts whose titles reflect a classification of entities as eighty-four can be found in "New Catalogus Catalogorum," volume 6: 307.

are not only mentioned in Yoga texts but also in Kāmaśāstra.[62] It is therefore apparent that the number eighty-four traditionally signifies completeness, and in some cases, sacredness. Multiples of the number eighty-four are also in use. The number 84,000, therefore, is frequent in Buddhist literature and stands for an extraordinary large and complete number: 84,000 *stūpas* are said to have been built by Aśoka, one each for the relics of the Buddha, and there are references to 84,000 kinds of enlightenment through Amitābha (Reck 1997: 548).

5.3 Eighty-four Āsanas in Older Texts

5.3.1 Haṭharatnāvalī

Underscoring the purely mystical nature of the number eighty-four, Shashibhusan Dasgupta (1976: 205) remarks: "We do not find ... these eighty-four *Āsanas* described anywhere, only a few of them being described in the Yogic and Tāntric literature." However, this statement turns out to be inaccurate. Although none of the extant older Yoga texts enumerate or describe eighty-four *āsanas*, two texts have been published which list or describe eighty-four Yoga postures. The earliest text is the Haṭharatnāvalī (HR) by Śrīnivāsa from Āndhra, South India, a Sanskrit text which can tentatively be dated to between 1625 and 1695 CE. The HR is strongly influenced by the Haṭhapradīpikā, which it frequently quotes. The names of the eighty-four postures, beginning with Siddhāsana and ending with Śavāsana, are enumerated in HR2 3.9–20 (see Appendix 8.1), but only thirty-six of the postures are described. In the list of postures, four varieties of the important lotus posture (6–9) are found. Their names differ from the five variations of the posture found in lists 8.3 and 8.4. There are as many as six different kinds of Mayūrāsana (10–15) and five kinds of Kukkuṭāsana (56–60). The peacock posture (Mayūrāsana), which figures prominently also in other lists of eighty-four postures, must have been considered especially important. Three varieties each of the Matsyendrāsana (25–27) and the Kūrmāsana (47–49) are listed. Many *āsana* names are uncommon and not found in other lists.

---

[62] See the list from the Kokaśāstra cited in Haṇmaṃte 1980: 553.

5.3.2 Jogapradīpakā

The only older text known so far which actually describes eighty-four *āsanas* is the North Indian Jogapradīpakā (JP) by Jayatarāma, a resident of Vṛndāvan, who wrote the work in 1737. Jayatarāma was a disciple of Payaharibābā, also called Kṛṣṇadāsa, who occupied the seat of Galta (Jaipur). The language of the JP is a mixed Hindī with Braj Bhāṣā, Kharī Bolī and semi-Sanskritic forms. The JP is clearly influenced by Svātmārāma's Haṭhapradīpikā. The names of the *āsanas* in this text, which are listed in Appendix 8.2, differ considerably from those listed in the Haṭharatnāvalī. They appear to have been compiled from disparate sources and also include two *mudrās*, Mahāmudrā āsana and Jonimudrā/Yonimudrā āsana. In section 5 of the text twenty-four *mudrās* are described separately. A comparatively large number of postures are named after Siddhas (12, 52–58). Some *āsana* names are Sanskrit, while others are derived from local languages. A summary of the descriptions of most of the eighty-four *āsanas* in section 3 of the JP can be found in Gharote's English introduction to his edition of the text (pp. 3–18). As Gharote notes, seventy of the eighty-four *āsanas* are also described in the Yogāsanamālā, a text possibly authored by Jayatarāma as well and written in 1768. Twenty-six of the *āsanas* are described in a manuscript of the Haṭhapradīpikā from Jodhpur.[63] The *āsanas* in the Jogapradīpakā differ considerably from those in the other traditions listed in the Appendices. Standing postures are completely absent. The performance of most *āsanas* is accompanied by the fixation of the gaze (*dṛṣṭi*) either on the tip of the nose or in between the eyebrows. Some *āsanas* are combined with *prāṇāyāma* practices and are held for a long time. Thus Pachimatāṇa/Paścimatāṇa āsana (7) is recommended for a period of three to six hours and that of the Kapālī/Kapāli āsana (17), for three hours. Some of the descriptions in the text bear a similarity to postures depicted in the sources in the Jodhpur tradition reproduced

[63] In the appendix to his edition of the JP, Gharote has included line drawings of sixty *āsanas*. These drawings were not commissioned to accompany the descriptions in the JP but to illustrate the *āsanas* in the Yogāsanamālā. Gharote informed me that the line drawings are taken from manuscript 5450 of the Yogāsanamālā preserved in the Rājasthān Oriental Research Institute, Jodhpur; it is currently being edited by him. According to Gharote, the illustrations are fairly reliable but need corrections in the light of the descriptions. The illustrations of the *āsanas* in the Yogāsanamālā reproduced in the appendix to Gharote's edition of the JP, however, appear to be not the original drawings of the eighteenth-century manuscript but a redrawn version. It should also be noted that they seem to have been taken from more than one source.

in section 6.4 of this book. The eighty-four *āsanas* according to the JP are illustrated in a set of circa nineteenth-century coloured drawings by an unknown artist which is described in section 6.2.1 and reproduced in section 6.2.2 of this book.

5.4 Eighty-four Āsanas in Contemporary Sources

5.4.1 Hanūmān Śarmā

In this section I will discuss several contemporary sets of eighty-four *āsanas* which I could identify.[64] Their names are listed in the Appendices. Selected sets of eighty-four *āsanas* are then reproduced in section 6 from extant drawings or photographs.

A mere list of the names of eighty-four postures along with remarks on their health benefits can be found in Daniélou's book "Yoga: The Method of Re-Integration" (1949: 146–149, Appendix C). As is often the case in his writings, Daniélou neglects to acknowledge his sources. However, a similar list of *āsana* names appears in the reference work "Saṃkhyā-Saṃket Koś," compiled by Haṇmaṃte in Marāṭhī (= Haṇmaṃte 1980: 553–554). This work identifies the Yogāṅka of the Hindī magazine Kalyāṇ published from Gorakhpur as the list's source. This piece of information enabled me to identify Hanūmān Śarmā's article "Yogavidyā: Āsan aur unkā upayog," published in Kalyāṇ no. 10 in September 1935, as the source of Daniélou's and Haṇmaṃte's lists of *āsanas*. The article includes a list of eighty-four *āsanas* with remarks on their health benefits but not a description of the postures. The origin of the list of names is not discussed. The *āsana* names are reproduced in Appendix 8.3 on the basis of Śarmā's list, with occasional variants found in Daniélou 1949 and Haṇmaṃte 1980 indicated in the notes. An interesting feature of this list is that it includes five varieties of Padmāsana (3–7), four of which are identical with those in list 8.4. Several *āsana* names in the list are reminiscent of types of *prāṇāyāma* (15, 16, 28).

5.4.2 Gaṅgādharan Nair

Two modern publications in Indian vernaculars that include sets of eighty-four *āsanas*

[64] Chidananda 1984: 96 refers to a publication titled "Yogasanas Illustrated" by Swami Shivananda, published "nearly fifty years ago in Madras." In it eighty-four important *āsanas* are supposed to be outlined. I was unable to locate a copy of the book.

have come to my attention. The first is a book by Gaṅgādharan Nair (1962)[65] of the Yogāsanakendram in Quilon, Kerala, which describes eighty-four *āsanas* based on a tradition from Kerala, about which no further information is provided. Their names are listed in Appendix 8.4. The set includes five kinds of Padmāsana (1, 2, 14, 15, 51), four of which are identical with types of Padmāsana in list 8.3. This is the only list that includes an 'energy lock' (*bandha*), namely Uḍḍiyānabandha (84), among the eighty-four *āsanas*. Seventy-one of the eighty-four *āsanas* are documented in photographs, *āsanas* 6, 7, 8, 10–12, 15, 17–19, 24, 41 and 55 not being illustrated. The photographs of the postures could not be reproduced here because of their poor quality.

5.4.3 Svāmī Svayamānanda

Svāmī Svayamānanda 1992 describes eighty-four *āsanas* from a different tradition. Eighty-one of these are accompanied by contemporary line drawings, which are reproduced in section 6.5. Their names are listed in Appendix 8.5. The three *āsanas* which are not illustrated are 9, 15 and 22. The author does not provide information about the origins of the set. The *āsanas* are arranged in a very systematic order, in which a basic posture is followed by its variation (for example, Sarvāṅgāsana, Ardhasarvāṅgāsana; Vajrāsana, Suptavajrāsana).

It is difficult to judge a tradition of postures merely on the basis of a posture sequence published in a book. Āsana practice is likely to show deviations from the written model, especially insofar as it includes or substitutes variations on the postures. We can see this clearly in the *āsana* sequence of the Yoga Challenge® System, which is addressed in the next section.

5.4.4 The Yoga Challenge® System

Antonio ('Tony') Sanchez, the founder and director of the United States Yoga Association (USYA) (1984–2005), now based in Cabo San Lucas, Baja, Mexico, teaches a system of Yoga called Yoga Challenge®. It consists of four segments (I–IV) of

[65] The original edition of 1962 was reprinted in 1966, 1971 and 1998. The 1998 edition by Imprint Books, Kollam, Kerala (labelled First Imprint Edition) differs somewhat from the 1962 edition in that it inserts some additional photographs and replaces some of the older

increasing difficulty. Yoga Challenge® IV includes a set of eighty-four *āsanas*, documented on a poster printed in 2003. The names of the *āsanas* are listed in Appendix 8.6 as printed on the poster, and photographs of the postures are reproduced in section 6.6. A video recording of Yoga Challenge® IV, released in 2001,[66] documents a total of 144 postures, which include the eighty-four postures and a number of variations not seen on the poster. The sequence of the postures in the video recording differs somewhat from that seen on the poster in its second part, where at times it follows the sequence in a list of ninety-one postures from Ghosh's College (see below).

Sanchez began his Yoga training in 1976 with Bikram Choudhury, a student of Bishnu Charan Ghosh (see below), in Beverly Hills, California. In 1979 he was certified by Ghosh's College of Physical Education in Calcutta (Kolkata), India. Ghosh's College was established in 1923 by Bishnu Charan Ghosh (1903–1970), who had been trained at the Yogoda Satsanga Brahmacharya Vidyalaya, a school for boys in Ranchi, Bihar. The school was started in 1917 by his older brother, Paramahansa Yogananda (1893–1952), who later founded the Self-Realization Fellowship in America. Ghosh also worked with Swami Shivananda Saraswati (1887–1963). The eighty-four postures in Yoga Challenge® IV are based on the curriculum taught at Ghosh's College, which is now under the directorship of Bishnu Charan Ghosh's son, Biswanath ('Bisu') Ghosh.

The only teaching material from Ghosh's College that was accessible to me is an older list of ninety-one 'advanced *āsanas*.' Sanchez received the list from his teacher Bikram Choudhury in the 1970s. In addition to ninety-one postures, the list includes four *mudrās*, five *bandhas*, four *kriyās* and two *prāṇāyāmas*. Śavāsana, which forms posture 37 in Sanchez's poster, is not counted separately in the list of ninety-one postures, although it appears several times in the list. Handwritten remarks in the list occasionally insert additional postures and renumber some of them. Sanchez explains that some of the ninety-one postures were treated as variants and not counted separately. We have no further information about the origins of the ninety-one *āsanas*

---

ones. However, in general the quality of the photographs is inferior to those reproduced in the 1962 edition.

[66] Yoga Challenge® IV: Hatha Yoga with Tony Sanchez. San Francisco, California: United States Yoga Association, 2001. VHS; 164 minutes.

in the list. It is quite possible that its compiler did not initially intend to make a list of eighty-four *āsanas* but that the postures were formed into such a system over time to honour the number eighty-four. Ghosh may have compiled the list himself by incorporating *āsanas* from traditions he was familiar with. Some of the original names clearly show traces of their North Indian derivation—for example, in the use of the letter *b* instead of *v* (Bibhaktahastatulādaṇḍāsana for Vibhaktahastatulādaṇḍāsana).

The eighty-four *āsanas* include four varieties of the lotus posture (Padmāsana, 27–30), which are similar to varieties of the postures in lists 8.3 and 8.4. There are also four kinds of peacock postures (Mayūrāsana, 73–76). This is the only list of eighty-four *āsanas* I found which includes the Sun Salutation (Sūryanamaskāra) (2).

Because of the considerable popularity of the Sun Salutation in modern Yoga practice, a few remarks about it may be appropriate here. The Sun Salutation is a separate set of postures, of which many different versions are known.[67] It may have been an independent exercise sequence which became linked to sun worship at some point in time. The Sun Salutation as taught, for example, by the Bihar School of Yoga features twelve postures, each accompanied by the recitation of a specific mantra which invokes one aspect of the sun god with a specific name.[68] Twelve, the number of the months of the solar cycle, is traditionally the symbolic number of the sun. The sequence of the Bihar School of Yoga begins with the practitioner standing with his palms joined together in front of this chest in salutation of the sun. After a sequence of postures, he performs the eight-limbed prostration (*aṣṭāṅganamaskāra*) to the sun, which is the climax of this sequence. In the eight-limbed prostration, the eight body parts of the practitioner (the forehead or chin, chest, both hands, knees and feet) touch the ground. This type of prostration is traditionally performed in India only by males. According to tradition, the sun god likes to be worshipped by prostrations. Some postures appear twice in the set: once when the practitioner moves into the prostration and—in reverse order—when he moves out of it. The twelve positions of the Sun

[67] Stenhouse 2001 describes twenty-three variations of the Sun Salutation, but there are more variants which are not included in her book.

[68] For a description, see, for example, Satyananda Saraswati 1983: 12–22, 41–46, 118–120. Dhirendra Brahmachari 1970: 283 refers to a Sun Salutation consisting of sixteen postures, which correspond to the sixteen aspects (*kalā*) of the sun. Pratinidhi 1939 divides the Sun Salutation into ten stages. K. Pattabhi Jois teaches one version with nine movements and a second version with seventeen.

Salutation are repeated twice, using alternate legs to complete a full round. Some of the postures in the series are also taught independently as *āsanas* in their own right. Although—contrary to popular claims—the Sun Salutation is not referred to in ancient Yoga texts and is unlikely to be a very ancient practice, it has enjoyed popularity as a physical exercise in India for several centuries.[69] In India, Sun Salutation competitions—referred to as Sūryanamaskār Yajñas in Hindī or as Sūryanamaskār Marathons—are held; during them young people repeat the sequence for hundreds or even thousands of times. In the photographs of the Sun Salutation in the Yoga Challenge® system, the sequence is broken down into twenty postures (2.1–2.20).[70] Like the two versions of the Sun Salutation of Jois's Aṣṭāṅgayoga, the set does not include the eight-limbed prostration. One of the postures, 2.3 (= 2.18), is included separately as the half moon posture (Ardhacandrāsana) (4) in the set of eighty-four postures.

A selection from the postures taught at Ghosh's College makes up the standard *āsana* sequence of Bikram Yoga™. This system, taught by Bikram Choudhury (b. 1946), founder of the worldwide Bikram's Yoga College of India™, features twenty-six *āsanas*. Table 1 shows correspondences between

1) the ninety-one *āsanas* taught at Ghosh's College, documented in an unpublished list from the 1970s, which I obtained from S. Wong/Sanchez (left-hand column),

2) the eighty-four postures as documented in a poster and taught by Sanchez as part of Yoga Challenge® IV (centre column) and

3) the postures taught in Bikram Yoga™ as published in Choudhury 1978 (right-hand column).

[69] Rāmdās, the seventeenth-century saint from Mahārāṣtra, is credited with reviving and spreading the practice of the Sun Salutation. He is supposed to have practised 1,200 Sun Salutations daily (Mujumdar 1950: 18–19, 453). For the role of Bhavanrao Pant, the Raja of Aundh, in propagating the Sun Salutation, see Mujumdar 1950: 452–456, Alter 1992: 98–103 and Alter 2000: 83–112. For a description of the practice in Mahārāṣtra, see Kuvalayananda 1926: 210.

[70] Some of these movements are identical; see 2.2 = 2.17 = 2.19; 2.3 = 2.18 (see also 4); 2.5 = 2.16; 2.6 = 2.15; 2.9 = 2.11.

TABLE 1

Comparative Overview of the *āsana*s Taught at Ghosh's College; by A. Sanchez as Part of Yoga Challenge® IV; and in Bikram Yoga™

Ghosh's List	Sanchez's Poster	Bikram Yoga™[71]
'Breathing', added to the list by a later hand	Not in poster but included in video documentation	1 Standing Deep Breathing ('Pranayama Series')
1–2	1–2 (see Appendix 8.6)	–
3 Pārśvārdhacandrāsana 4 Ardhacandrāsana 5 Pādahastāsana	3 Pārśvārdhacandrāsana 4 Ardhacandrāsana 5 Pādahastāsana	2 Ardhacandrāsana, Pādahastāsana ('Ardha-Chandrasana with Pada-Hastasana')
6 Trikoṇāsana	6 Trikoṇāsana	9 Trikoṇāsana ('Trikanasana')
7 Daṇḍāyamānavibhakta-pādajānuśirāsana	7 Daṇḍāyamānavibhakta-pādajānuśirāsana	10 Daṇḍāyamānavibhaktapāda-jānuśirāsana ('Dandayamana-Bibhaktapada-Janushirasana')
8 Utkaṭāsana	8 Utkaṭāsana	3 Utkaṭāsana ('Utkatasana')
9 Garuḍāsana	9 Garuḍāsana	4 Garuḍāsana ('Garurasana')
10 Daṇḍāyamānajānu-śirāsana	10 Daṇḍāyamānajānu-śirāsana	5 Daṇḍāyamānajānuśirāsana ('Dandayamana-Janushirasana')
11 Daṇḍāyamānadhanur-āsana	11 Daṇḍāyamānadhanur-āsana	6 Daṇḍāyamānadhanurāsana ('Dandayamana-Dhanurasana')
12 Tulādaṇḍāsana 13 Vibhaktahastatulādaṇḍā-sana	12 Tulādaṇḍāsana 13 Vibhaktahastatulādaṇḍā-sana	7 Tulādaṇḍāsana ('Tuladandasana')
14 Daṇḍāyamānavibhakta-pādapaścimottānāsana	14 Daṇḍāyamānavibhakta-pādapaścimottānāsana	8 Daṇḍāyamānavibhakta-pādapaścimottānāsana ('Dandayamana-Bibhaktapada-Paschimotthanasana')

[71] I have standardized and partially corrected the orthography of the *āsana* names so as to enable the reader to compare the names of the postures with those in other lists. The orthography of the names as printed in Choudhury 1978 is added in parentheses.

15 Tāḍāsana	15 Tāḍāsana	11 Tāḍāsana ('Tadasana')
16 Pādāṅguṣṭhāsana	16 Pādāṅguṣṭhāsana	12 Pādāṅguṣṭhāsana ('Padangustasana')
17–36	17–36 (see Appendix 8.6)	–
Not counted separately	37 Śavāsana	13 Śavāsana ('Savasana')
37 Pavanamuktāsana	38 Pavanamuktāsana	14 Pavanamuktāsana ('Pavanamuktasana')
Not counted separately	Not counted separately	15 Sit-Up
38 Bhujaṅgāsana	39 Bhujaṅgāsana	16 Bhujaṅgāsana ('Bhujangasana')
39 Śalabhāsana	40 Śalabhāsana	17 Śalabhāsana ('Salabhasana')
40 Pūrṇaśalabhāsana	41 Pūrṇaśalabhāsana	18 Pūrṇaśalabhāsana ('Poorna-Salabhasana')
41 Dhanurāsana	42 Dhanurāsana	19 Dhanurāsana ('Dhanurasana')
42 Suptavajrāsana	43 Suptavajrāsana	20 Suptavajrāsana ('Supta-Vajrasana')
43 Ardhakūrmāsana	44 Ardhakūrmāsana	21 Ardhakūrmāsana ('Ardha-Kurmasana')
44 Uṣṭrāsana	45 Uṣṭrāsana	22 Uṣṭrāsana ('Ustrasana')
45 Śaśakāsana	46 Śaśakāsana	23 Śaśakāsana ('Sasangasana')
46 Jānuśirāsana 47 Paścimottānāsana	47 Jānuśirāsana 48 Paścimottānāsana	24 Jānuśirāsana, Paścimottānāsana ('Janushirasana with Paschimotthanasana')
48–55	49–58 (see Appendix 8.6)	–
56 Ardhamatsyendrāsana	59 Ardhamatsyendrāsana	25 Ardhamatsyendrāsana ('Ardha-Matsyendrasana')
Kapālabhāti, included in a separate category of *prāṇāyāma*	Not in poster but included in video demonstration	26 Kapālabhāti ('Kapalbhati in Vajrasana')
57–91	60–84 (see Appendix 8.6)	–

Although the sequence of *āsanas* in Bikram Yoga™ differs occasionally and some minor modifications are seen, it is clear that it is based on the posture sequence taught at Ghosh's College, from which it is a selection. The two breathing exercises included in Bikram Yoga™ as 1 (Standing Deep Breathing) and 26 (Kapālabhāti in Vajrāsana) are also part of Yoga Challenge® IV and documented at the beginning and end of the video demonstration (but not in the poster). Ghosh's list of ninety-one postures adds Kapālabhāti in a separate category of *prāṇāyāma*. Bikram's 'sit-up' (15) is also included in Yoga Challenge® IV, where it is usually performed when moving out of Śavāsana. However, the sit-ups do not count as separate postures in the set of eighty-four postures. An innovation in Bikram Yoga™ is the mandatory hot temperature (around 100° F) in the Yoga studios.

6. Sets of Illustrations of Eighty-four Āsanas

6.1 Preliminary Remarks

While there is no shortage of publications featuring photographs of practitioners performing Yoga postures, few traditional illustrations of *āsanas* have been published. An important document is a set of drawings of 122 *āsanas* reproduced in Sjoman 1999. These drawings belong to the Mahārāṇī's manuscript of a version of the nineteenth-century Śrītattvanidhi, a work compiled by Mummaḍi Kṛṣṇarāja Wodeyar (1794–1868). The manuscript is preserved in the Sarasvatī Bhāṇḍār Library, the private library of the Mysore Palace, and dates back to between 1811 and 1868.[72] The descriptions of the *āsanas* are found in the ninth and last section of the manuscript, but do not form part of the recension of the text published by the Veṅkaṭeśvar Press. Since the Śrītattvanidhi is a compendium covering a wide range of topics information on additional topics a compiler considered important, such as Yoga postures, could have easily been interpolated into the text of this recension at a later stage. Sjoman also reproduces illustrations from a compilation of different texts on Yoga titled Haṭhayogapradīpikā (Sjoman 1999: 63), which is also preserved in manuscript form in the Sarasvatī Bhāṇḍār Library. This unpublished text is of unknown date and is different from Svātmārāma's Haṭhapradīpikā.

Also of interest is the set of seventy-four coloured drawings of (mostly) *āsanas* according to the Gheraṇḍa-Saṃhitā, purchased by R. Garbe in Vārāṇasī in 1886 and published in Schmidt 1908.

Line drawings of *āsanas* are included in a small book written in Marāṭhī language and published at the end of the nineteenth century. Its title can be translated as 'Eighty-four *āsanas* included in the Yoga with eight ancillary parts, with illustrations' (= Dharmasiṃha 1899). Although the title promises a description of eighty-four *āsanas*, the book includes descriptions and drawings of as many as ninety-seven *āsanas* with no sources indicated. Perhaps it was not the original author's

[72] This information is based on Sjoman 1999: 40, 35.

intention to present a set of eighty-four postures. It is also possible that in practice some of the ninety-seven postures were considered variants and not counted among the eighty-four. It could also be that someone expanded the list of eighty-four postures by adding new postures. The situation can perhaps be compared to cases of collections of 108 names of deities. When counted, these names are often not exactly 108. But traditional commentators on these texts will usually interpret them so as to make 108.

Among the unpublished illustrated manuscripts of interest in this context is a nineteenth-century "Illustrated Book of Yoga Postures" from Rājasthān, preserved in the Ajit Mookerjee Collection in the Tantra Art Gallery of the National Museum, New Delhi. A few drawings with text are reproduced in Mookerjee 1971, no. 358 and in Rawson 1973, plates 138–139. Also of interest are sets of miniature paintings of twenty-one *āsana*s in four manuscripts of the Persian Bahr al-Hayat, a text which appears to be a translation of a lost work in Sanskrit or Hindī titled Amṛtakuṇḍa ('Pool of Nectar').[73] The oldest of these manuscripts dates from 1600–1605 and is kept in the Chester Beatty Library, Dublin (Leach 1995: 556–564). The other three manuscripts are based on it.

Traditional sets of drawings of eighty-four *āsana*s are rare. In this book I reproduce two complete sets from the nineteenth century. The most important one illustrates the eighty-four *āsana*s according to the Jogapradīpakā.

6.2 The Coloured Drawings of the Āsanas according to the Jogapradīpakā

6.2.1 A Description of the Drawings according to the Jogapradīpakā

It has long been known that coloured drawings of *āsana*s and *mudrā*s with accompanying text are kept in the British Library, London, and several of them have been published. However, the document has long remained unidentified and the complete set of drawings unpublished. The document is catalogued as manuscript Add. 24099 and labelled "Asanas and Mudras (Hata [sic] yoga)." According to a prefactory note by Sir Frederic Madden, who was the former keeper of the manuscript department of the British Library, Brigadier-Major H.E. Jerome of the 19th Regiment obtained the

[73] For the different versions of this text, see Ernst 2003. The four manuscripts are listed in Ernst 2003: 221, note 47.

manuscript from the library of the Rānī of Jhansi in central India "at the sacking of that place in April 1858" (Blumhardt 1899: 63) and donated it to the British Library on April 17, 1861. A brief description of it is found in a catalogue volume.[74] Losty describes it in an English article (1985), in which he reproduces twelve drawings in colour. The Italian version of the article (1985b) includes eighteen colour images. Nineteen coloured drawings can be viewed on the website of the British Library under "Images Online," shelfmark Add. 24099.

The document consists of 118 folios measuring 8 1/2 by 4 1/2 inches and includes the following material:

1) a coloured drawing of Śiva as an ascetic instructing a group of devotees, with Pārvatī seated on his left thigh (fol. 1);

2) a colour image of a four-armed Gaṇeśa with his consort (fol. 2), which can be viewed at:
http://www.bl.uk/collections/northindia.html#muscat_highlighter_first_match ("Hindi Asanas and Mudras (Yoga); portrait of Ganesha;" retrieved April 21, 2004);

3) eighty-four coloured drawings, numbered from 1 to 84, with accompanying text illustrating and describing eighty-four *āsanas* (fols. 3–86);

4) twenty-four coloured drawings illustrating and describing twenty-four *mudrās* (fols. 87–117);

5) and a coloured drawing of a perfected Yogin (fol. 118) showing the *kuṇḍalinī*, the *cakras* and deities populating his different body parts.

Losty 1985: 100 characterizes the drawings as executed in the Rajput style with elements of the Kangra idiom.[75] He assigns the manuscript to the Panjab and dates it to about 1830.

After comparing the names of the *āsanas* in the document with those in lists of names of eighty-four *āsanas* which I had prepared for this book, I was able to identify the text portions of this document as extracts from Jayatarāma's Jogapradīpakā (JP). This work was written in 1737 and is discussed in section 5.3.2. The text on fols. 3–86 of the document, which describes the eighty-four *āsanas*, can be shown to have been extracted from JP 7,2–36,2. The text on fols. 87–117, which describes the twenty-four

[74] See Blumhardt 1899: 63 (no. 96).
[75] Email communication dated April 21, 2004.

mudrās, was extracted from JP 53,9–71,14.

In this book the complete set of drawings of eighty-four *āsanas* is reproduced for the first time. It was obviously commissioned to illustrate the descriptions in the JP. If Losty's assumption is correct, it was prepared about one hundred years after the composition of the JP and testifies to the importance of this text.

The scribe must have copied the text of the JP from a manuscript which was not used by Gharote for his edition of the text. This would explain the occurrence of mostly minor textual variants which are not recorded in the apparatus to Gharote's edition of the JP. In the set of drawings Siddhi/Siddha āsana appears only once, as the last *āsana* in the series. In Gharote's edition this *āsana* is described twice (see Appendix 8.2, 13a and 84). Among the usually minor orthographic variants in the names of the postures, the manuscript offers the variant Veda āsana (31) for the reading Deva āsana in Gharote's edition.

The coloured drawings depict several Yogins, of bluish complexion and covered only with a loincloth, performing the *āsanas*. The practitioners of the two *mudrās* in this section (14, 15) and those of the twenty-four *mudrās* in the next section are yellowish. The Yogins have long hair, which is sometimes tied in a knot, and are frequently shown seated on a tiger or antelope skin, as traditionally recommended. They are often accompanied by an attendant of yellowish complexion, who is either standing by or performing chores. A lotus pond is frequently seen to the front, and a natural landscape with trees and occasionally buildings in the background.

In addition to the eighty-four coloured drawings, we find several line drawings below the textual descriptions, which show a Yogin performing the postures. They may be intended to correct errors in the way technical aspects of the postures are represented in the coloured drawings. The sketches have not been reproduced here, but they would need to be included in a study of the *āsana* section of the JP. Such a detailed comparison between the *āsana* descriptions of the JP and their representation in the drawings is not possible at this time and will have to wait until a critical edition of the JP becomes available.

6.2.2 A Reproduction of the Drawings according to the Jogapradīpakā (by permission of the British Library, Add. 24099)

1

2

3

4

5

6

7

8

9

10

11

12

13

14

15

16

17

18

19

20

21

22

23

24

25

26

27

28

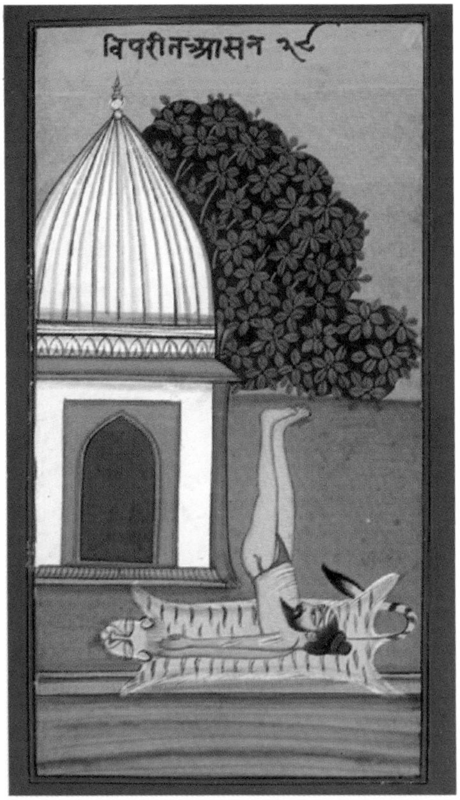
विपरीतआसन २९

29

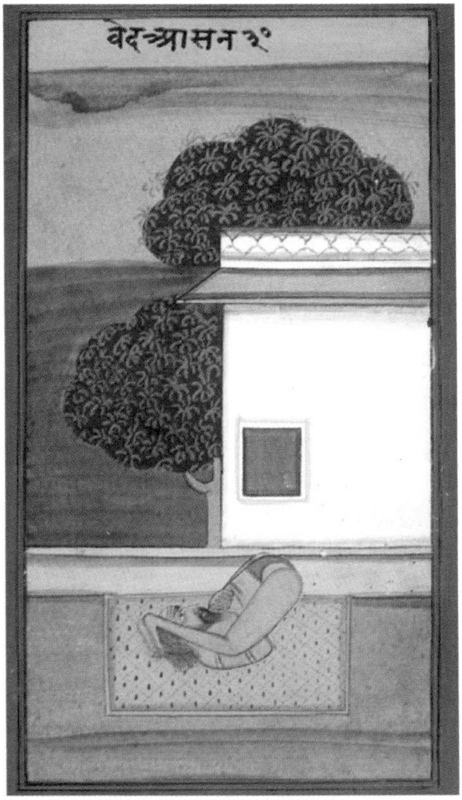
वेदआसन ३०

30

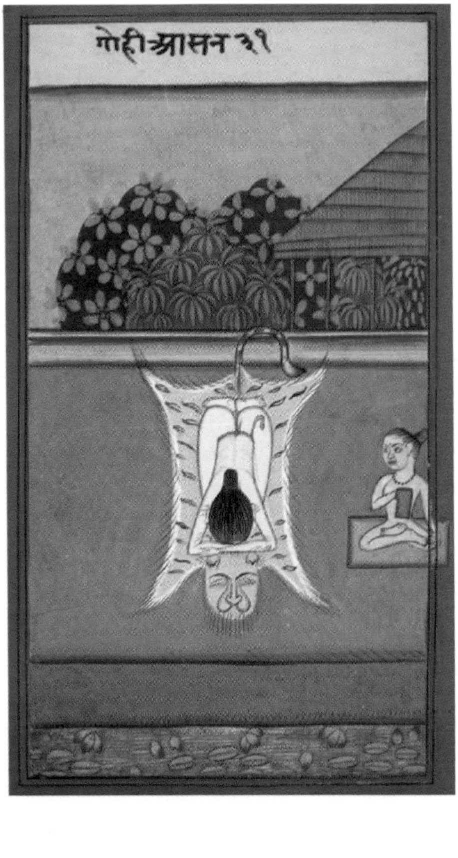
गोहीआसन ३१

31

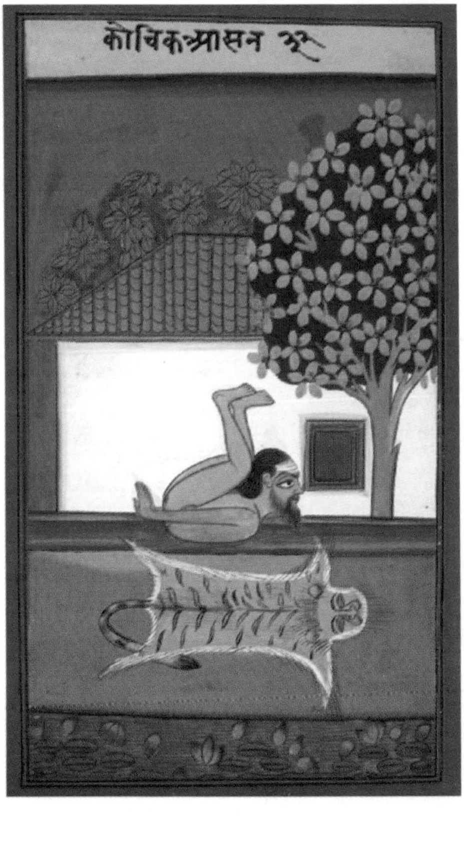
कौचिकआसन ३२

32

33

34

35

36

37

38

39

40

41

42

43

44

45

46

47

48

49

50

51

52

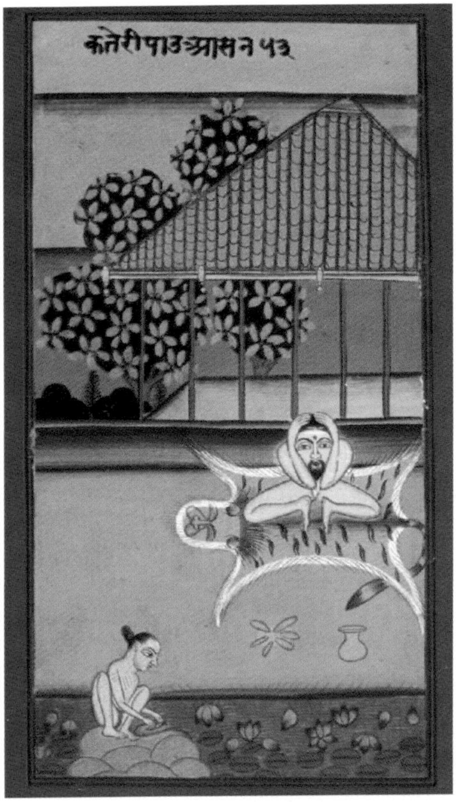

कतेरीपाउआसन ५३

53

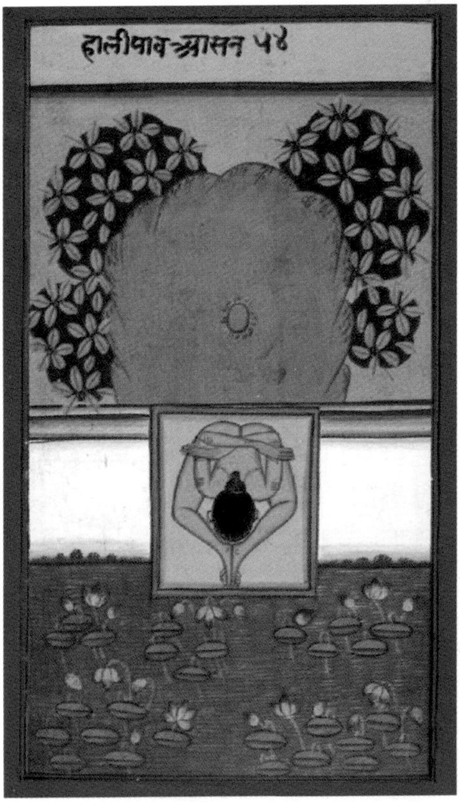

हालीपावआसन ५४

54

55

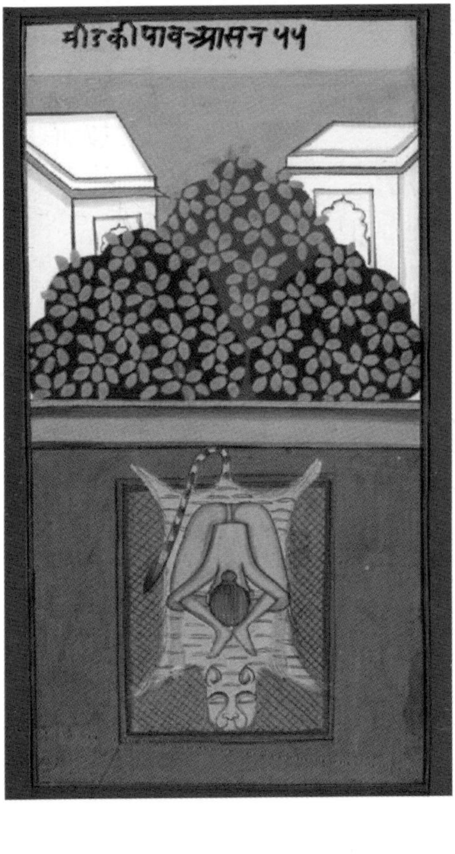

मीडकीपावआसन ५५

56

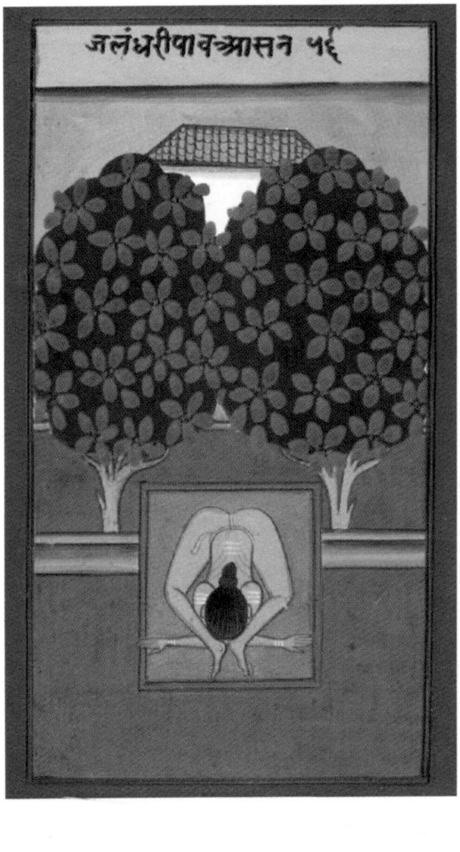

जलंधरीपावआसन ५६

57

58

59

60

61

62

63

64

65

66

67

68

69

70

71

72

73

74

75

76

77

78

79

80

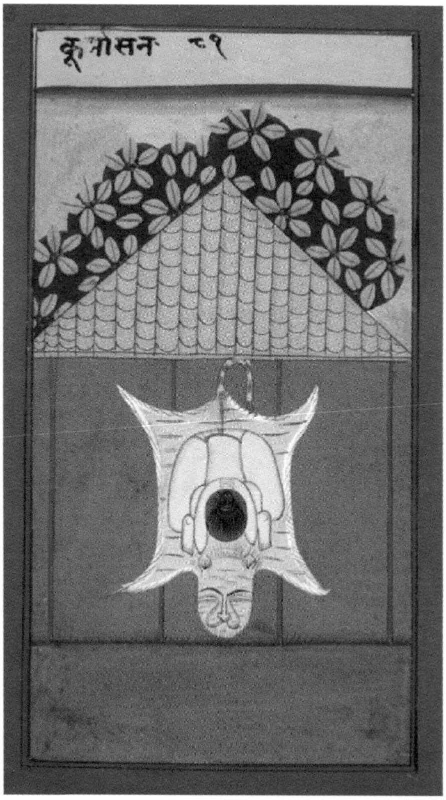

81

82

83

84

6.3 The Line Drawings from Nepal

6.3.1 A Description of the Line Drawings from Nepal

A set of traditional line drawings of eighty-four *āsanas* forms part of manuscript 347 preserved in the Keśar Library, Kathmandu.[76] It is a concertina-type manuscript (*thyā-saphū*) made of paper, which was coated with yellow pigment to protect it from insects. The manuscript consists of forty-eight folios and is labelled "Hastamudrā, caurāshī āsana," which means 'hand gestures, eighty-four *āsanas*.' The section on *āsanas* consists of fifteen folios, with an average of six line drawings per folio.

The circa nineteenth-century line drawings of the *āsanas* are reproduced in section 6.3.2 for the first time. They show different practitioners performing *āsanas*, numbered from one to eighty-four. Some sit on tiger skins and have moustaches. Some practitioners wear headgear, while others have long, unbound hair or hair tied into topknots. Some figures wear the sacred thread, and others a garland of *rudrākṣa* beads. A variety of postures are shown, some of which appear to be identical or almost identical with one another, such as 32 and 66, and 40 and 78. Many of the postures are known from works on Yoga, such as 14, which shows a practitioner performing the headstand with his legs in the lotus posture, or 65, which appears to show a practitioner in what is often termed the 'bound lotus posture.' It is, however, not possible to identify the *āsanas*, since no names are given in the manuscript, and different Yoga traditions label the postures differently. It would be meaningless to try to identify the postures with the help of descriptions in other texts, since we do not know anything about the tradition in which the drawings originated.

A similar but incomplete set of line drawings from Nepal is found on three and a half unnumbered folios in paper manuscript (*thyāsaphū*) 82.234 in the collection of the Newark Museum. An anonymous donor gifted this still unpublished manuscript to the museum in 1982. The line drawings, which are neither numbered nor labelled, correspond to drawings 1–6 and 15–53 in the Keśar Library manuscript. The set is not reproduced in this book since it is incomplete and the drawings not very refined.

---

76 A microfilm of the manuscript can be accessed through the Nepal-German Manuscript Preservation Project under reel number C 37/6.

It is possible that the Nepalese artist intended to portray the eighty-four Siddhas performing the eighty-four *āsanas*, as in the sources relating to the Jodhpur tradition (section 6.4), but this cannot be determined with any certainty. The representations of the Yogins resemble to some extent those of the Siddhas in Yogic postures portrayed in a circa fifteenth-century painting from western Tibet of Vajradhara surrounded by the Siddhas (Linrothe 2006: 220). The painting is now in the Collection of S. and D. Rubin, New York. The resemblance is clearly seen in those practitioners depicted bent forward and those with one or both legs extended.

6.3.2 A Reproduction of the Line Drawings from Nepal

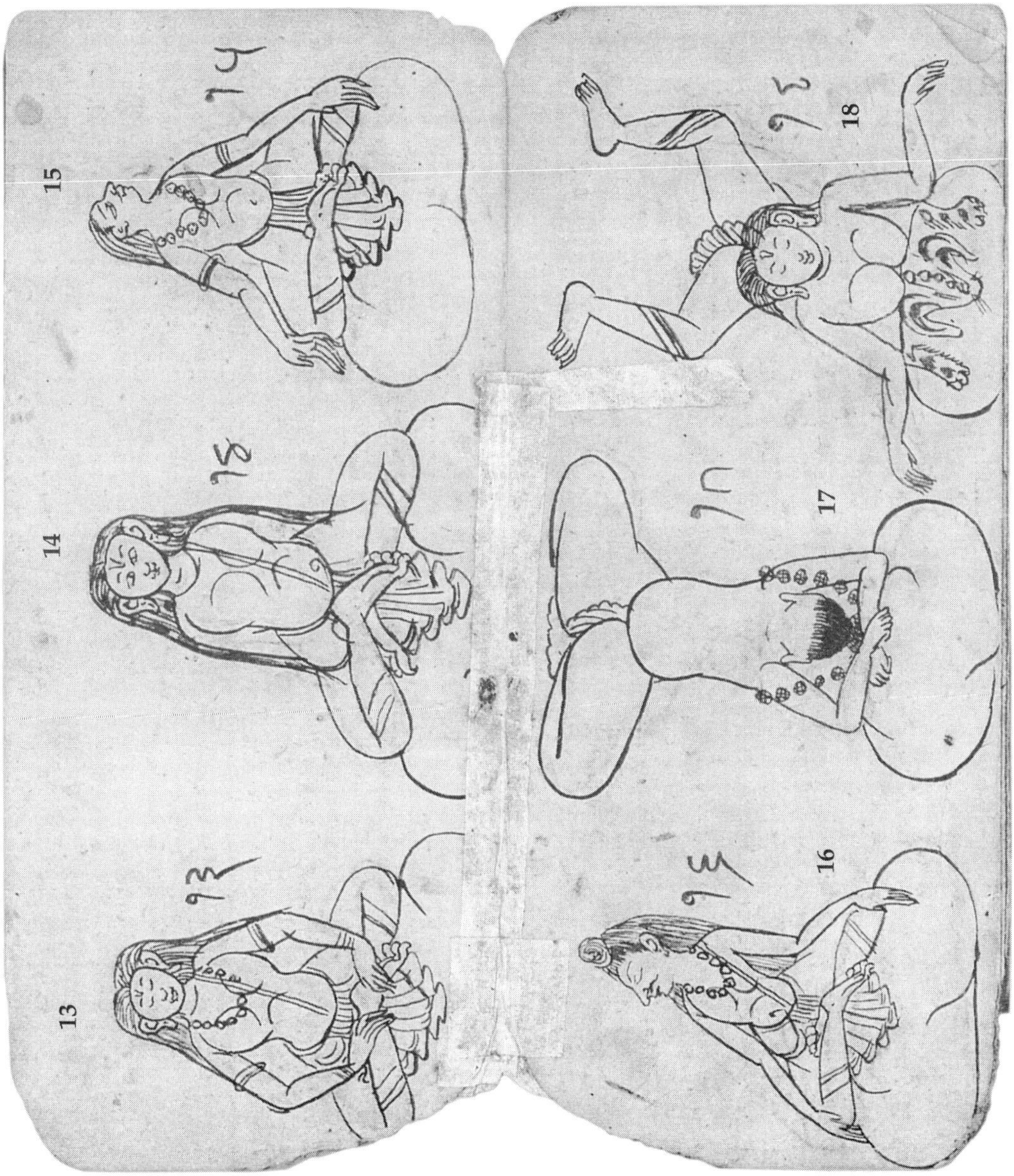
13
14
15
16
17
18

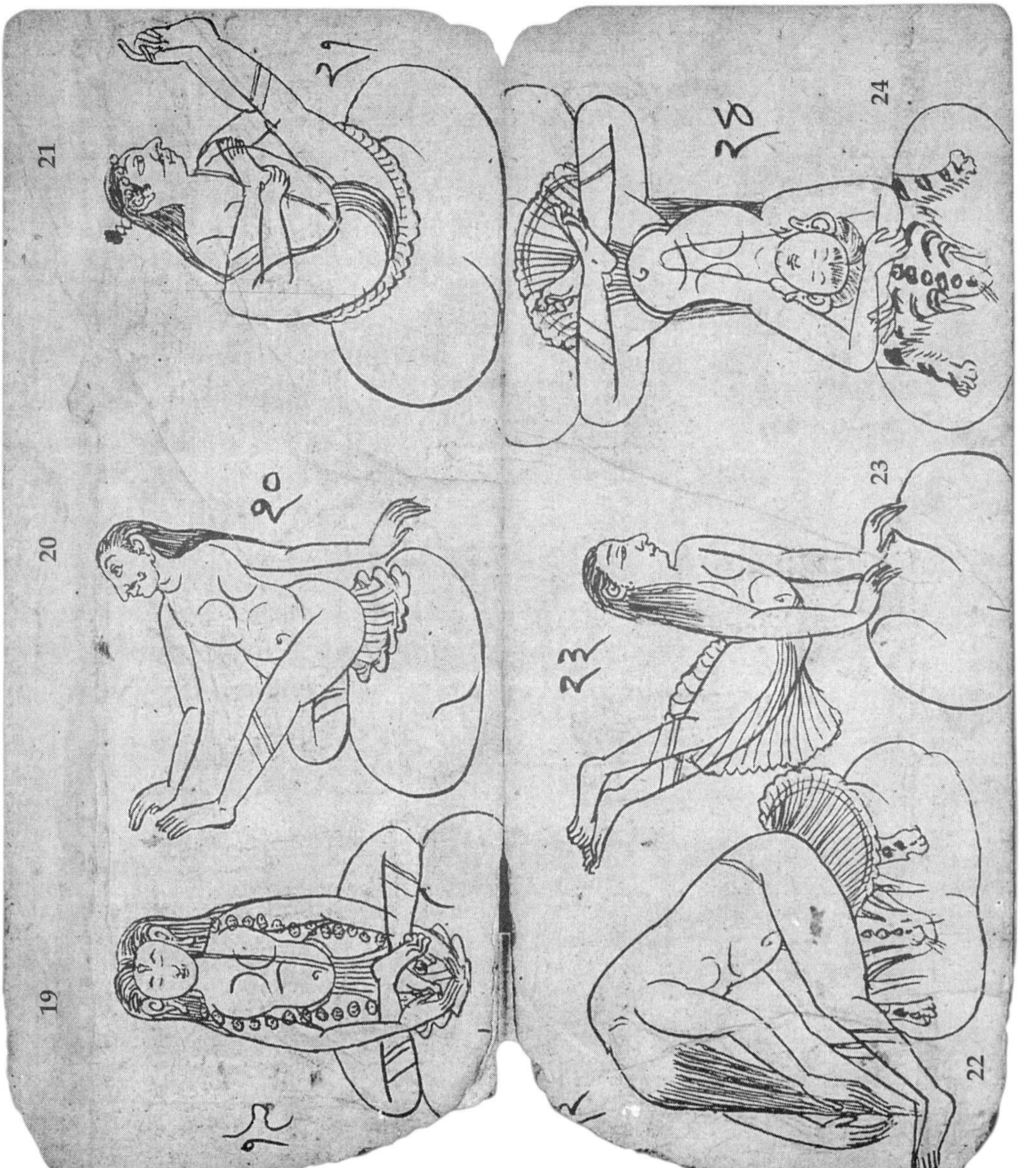
19
20
21
22
23
24

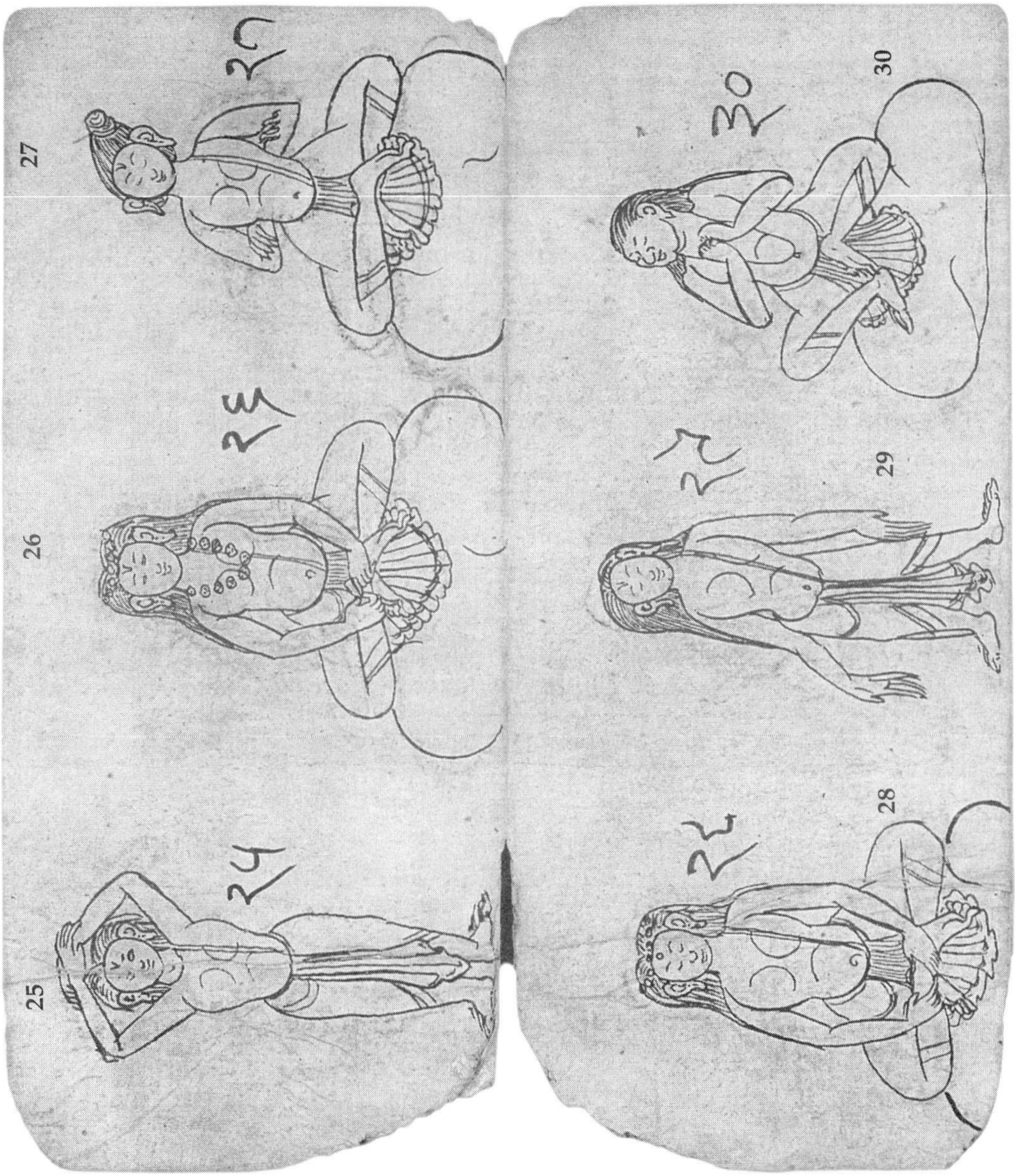
25
26
27
28
29
30

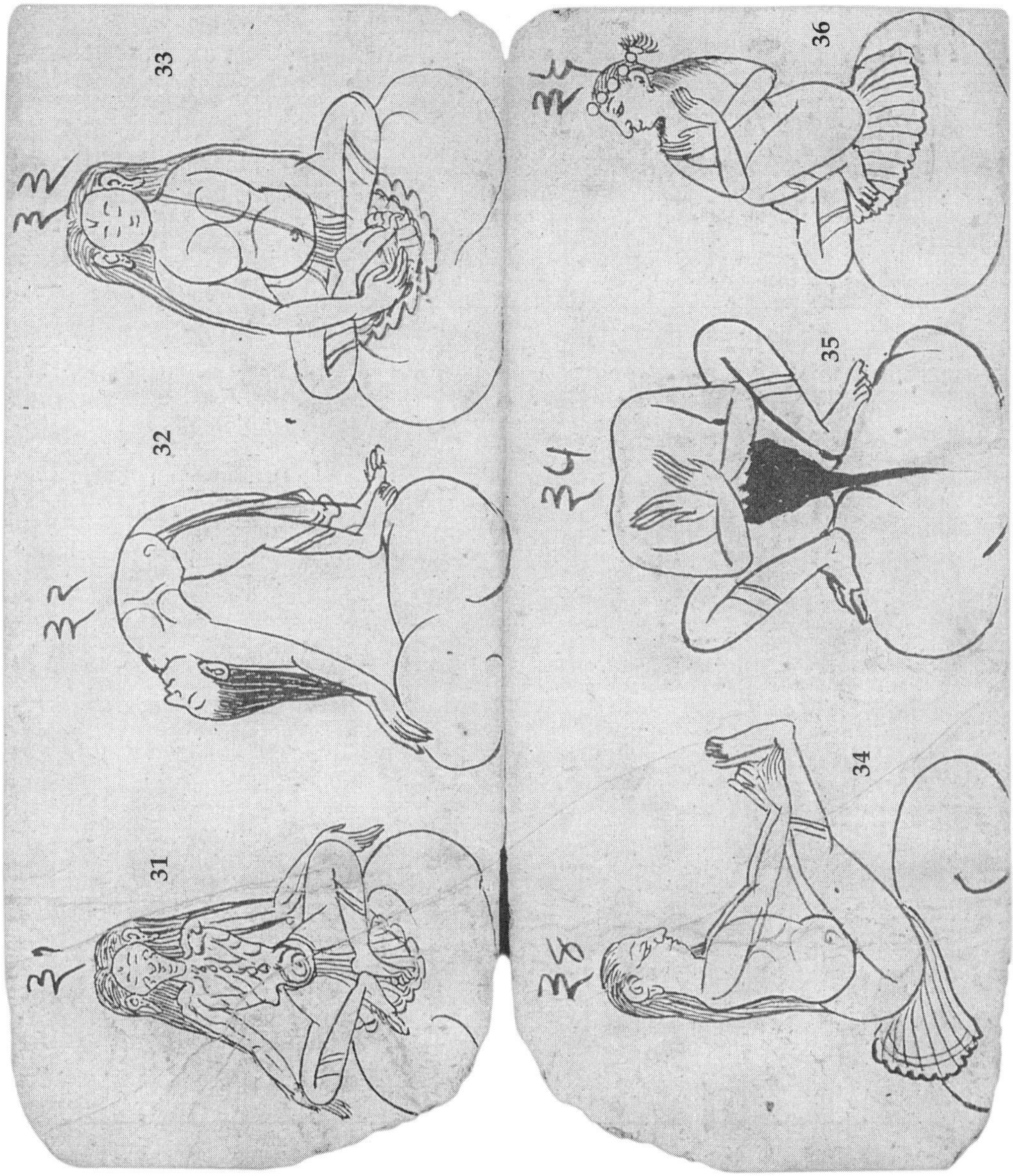
31
32
33
34
35
36

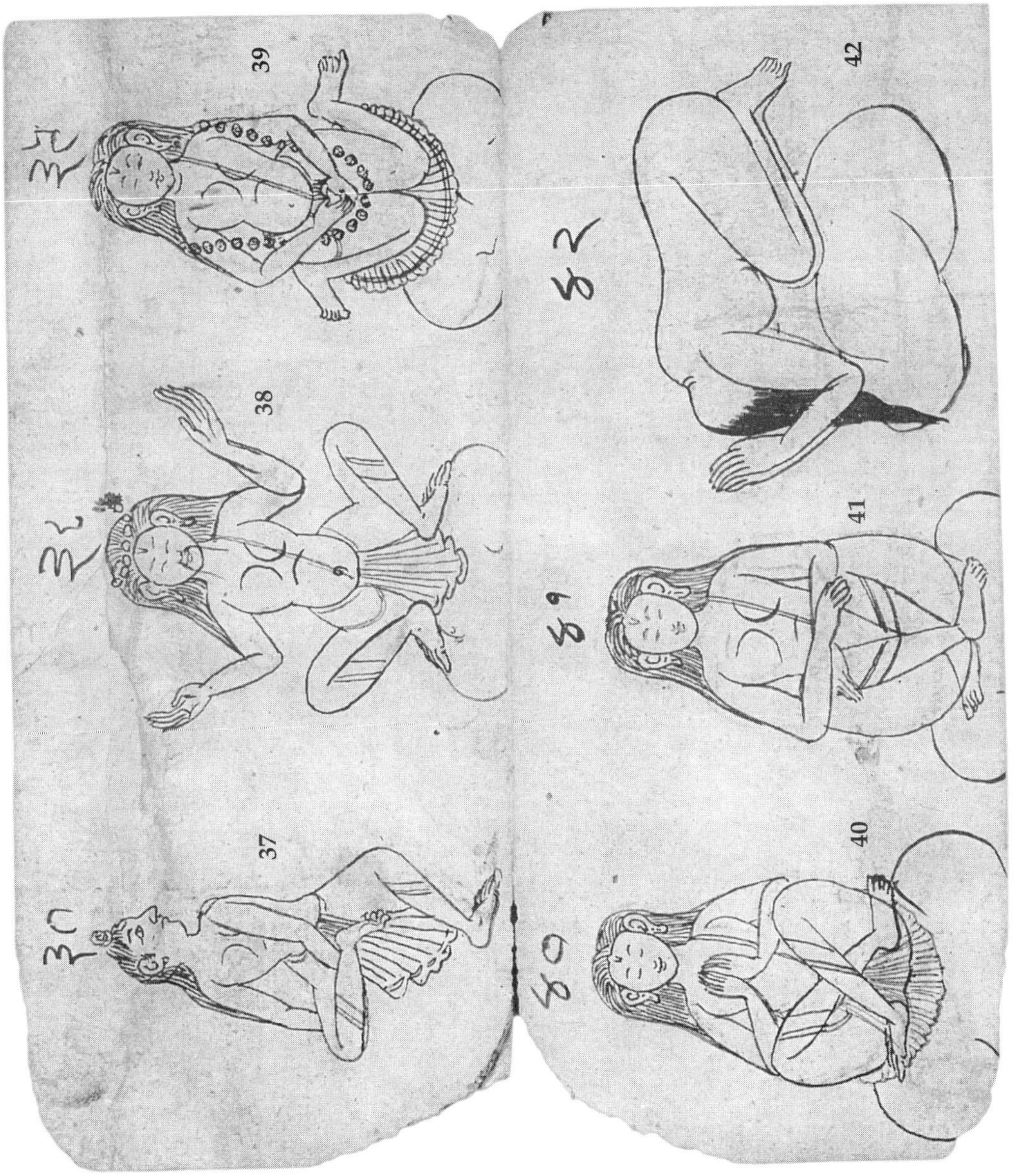
37
38
39
40
41
42

43
44
45
46
47
48

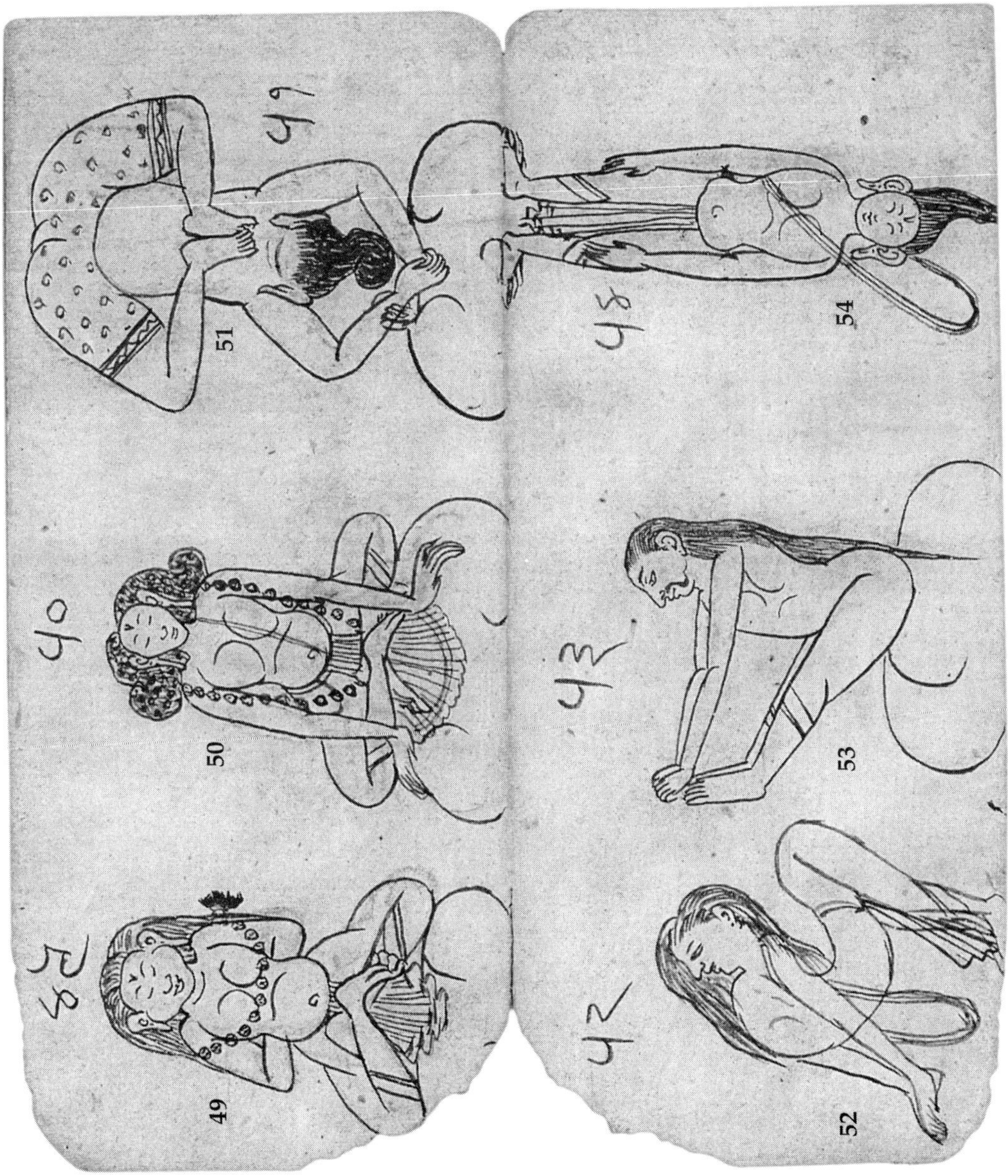
49
50
51
52
53
54

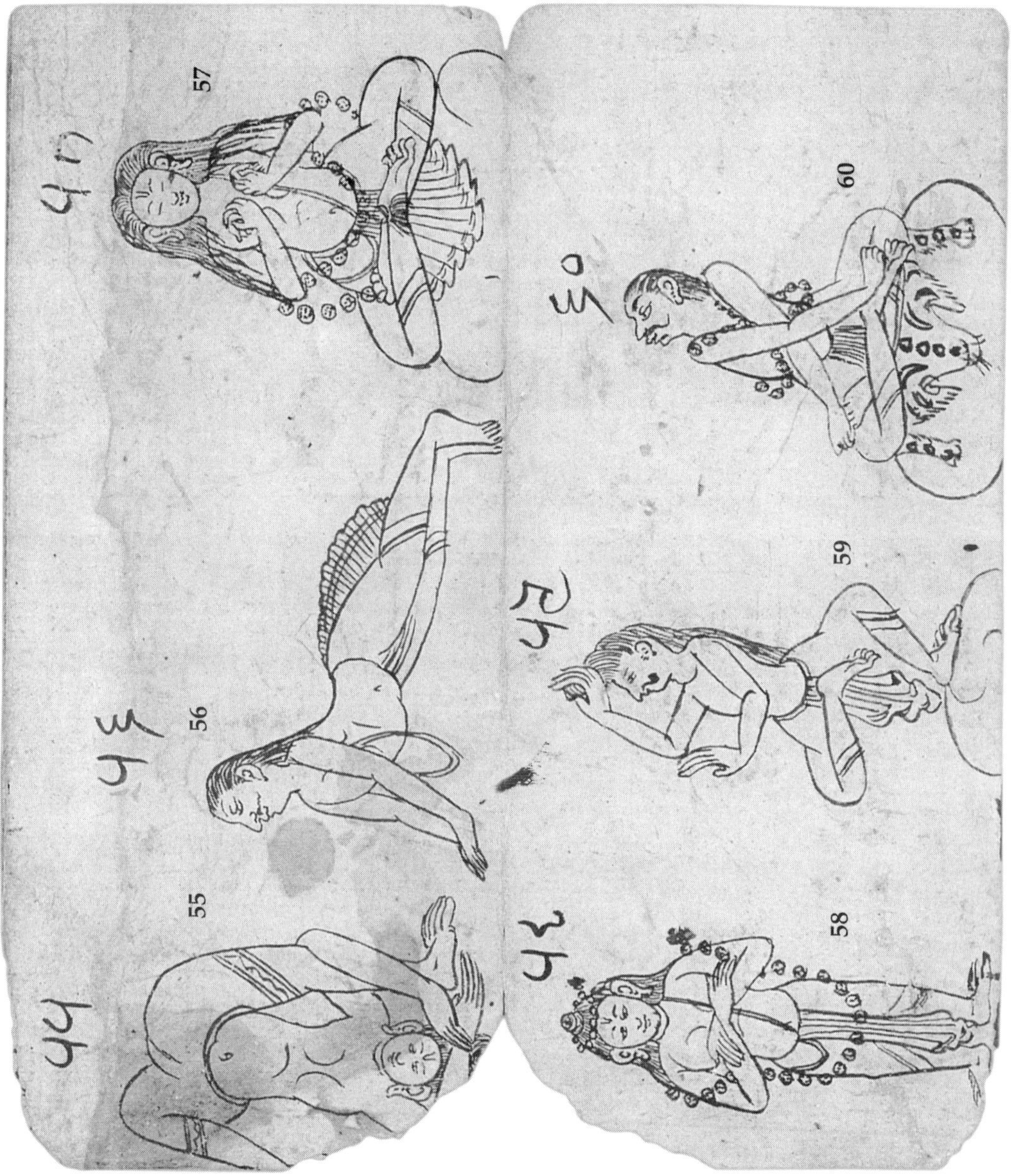
55
56
57
58
59
60

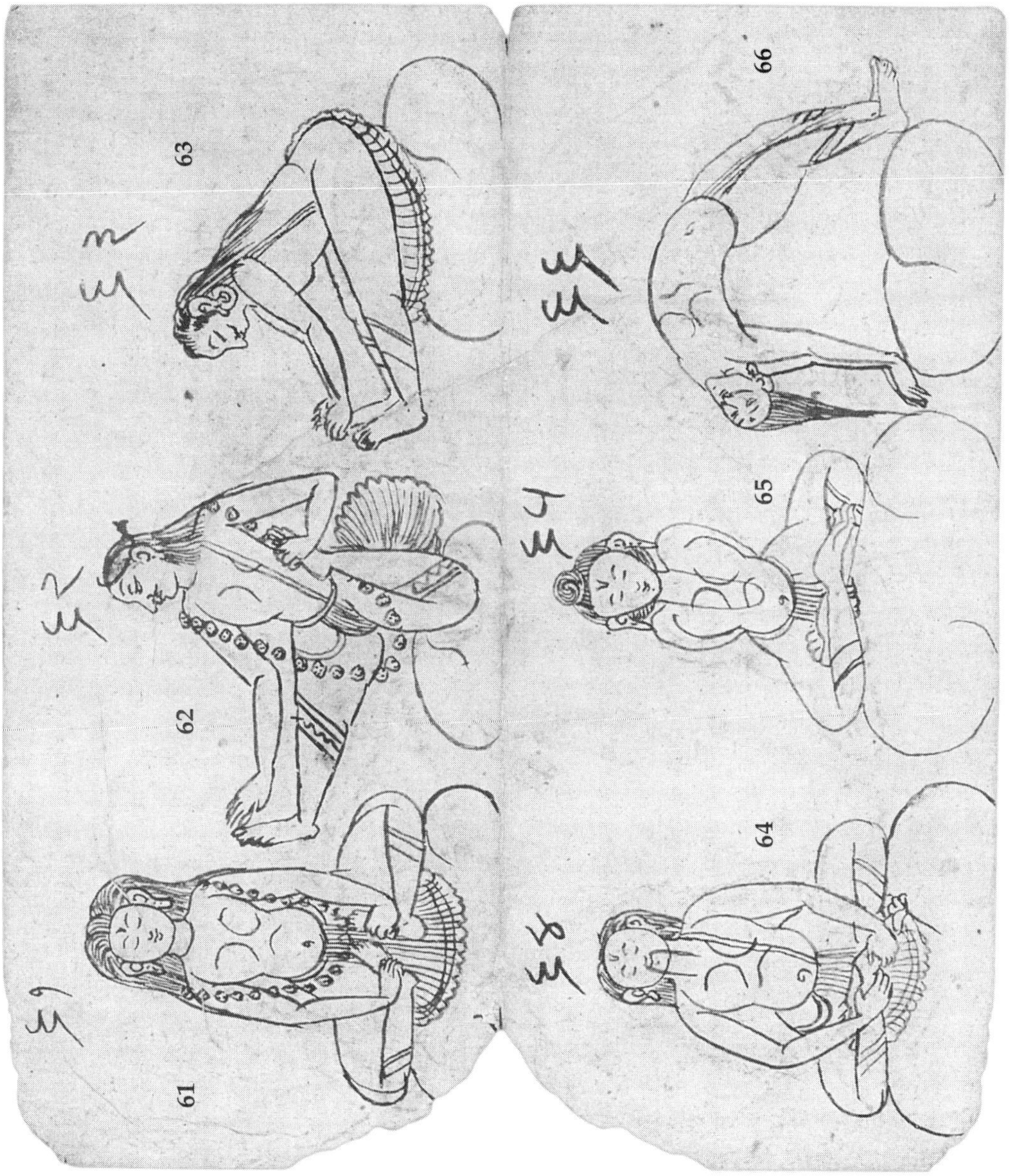
61
62
63
64
65
66

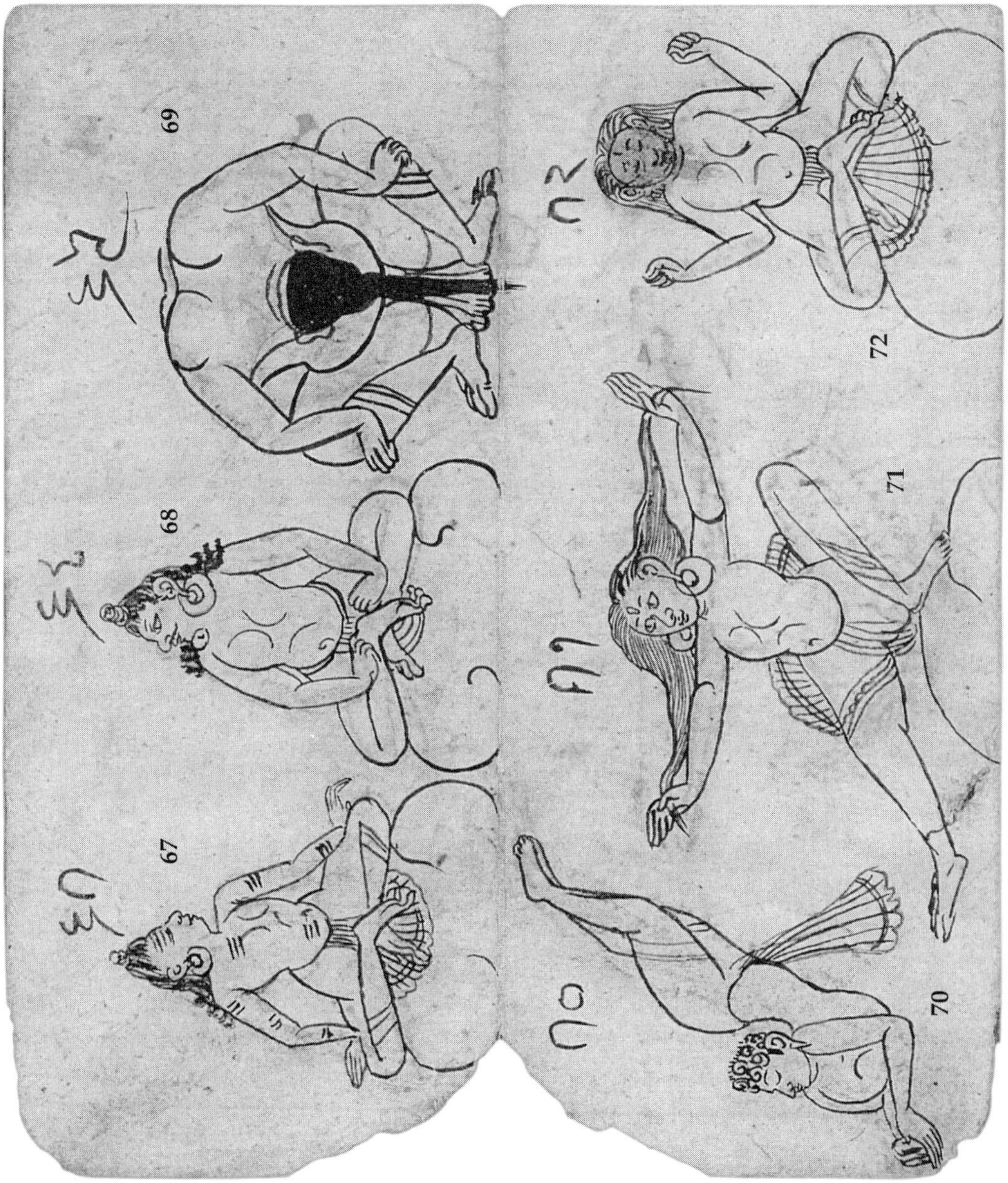
67
68
69
70
71
72

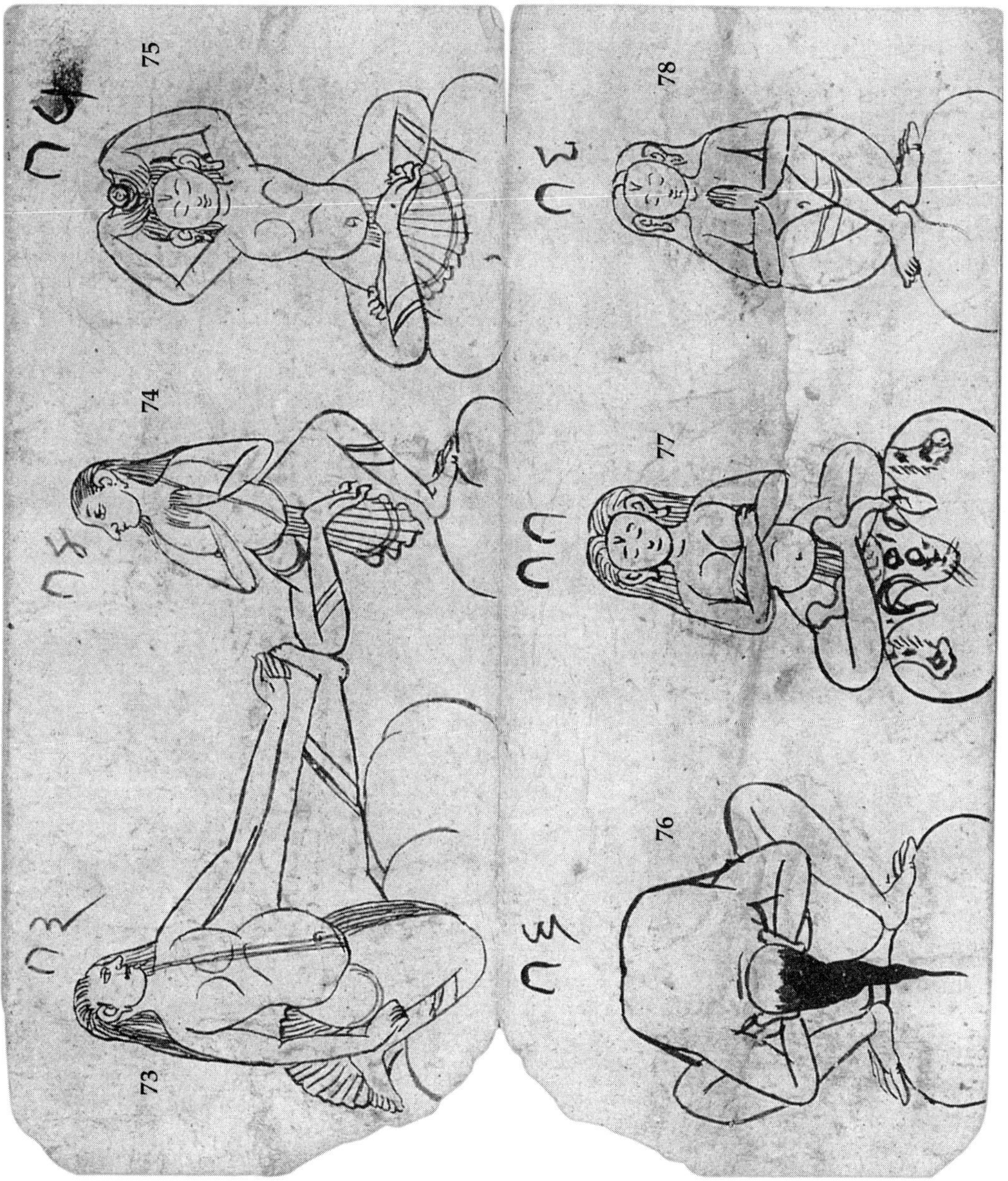
73
74
75
76
77
78

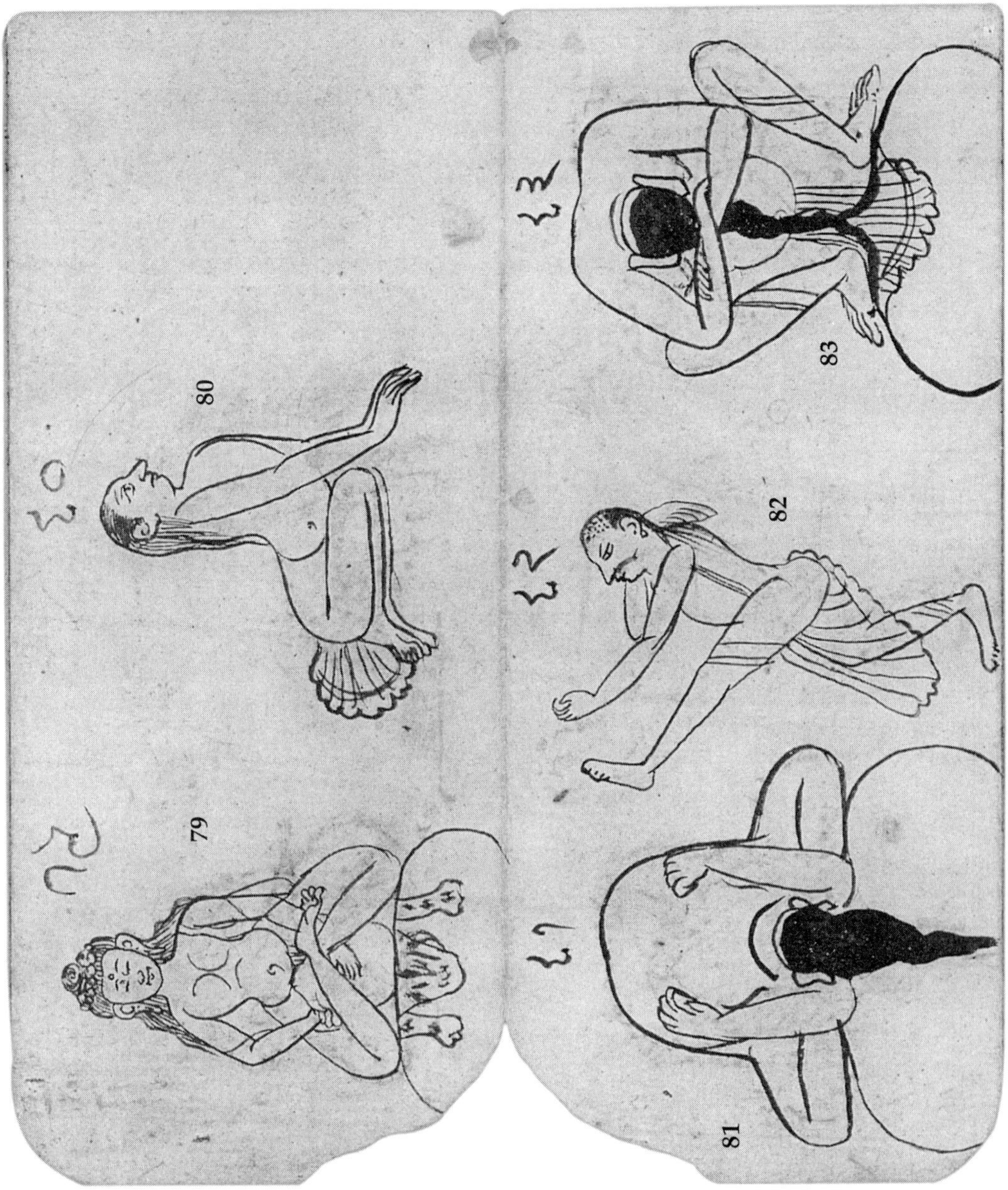
79
80
81
82
83

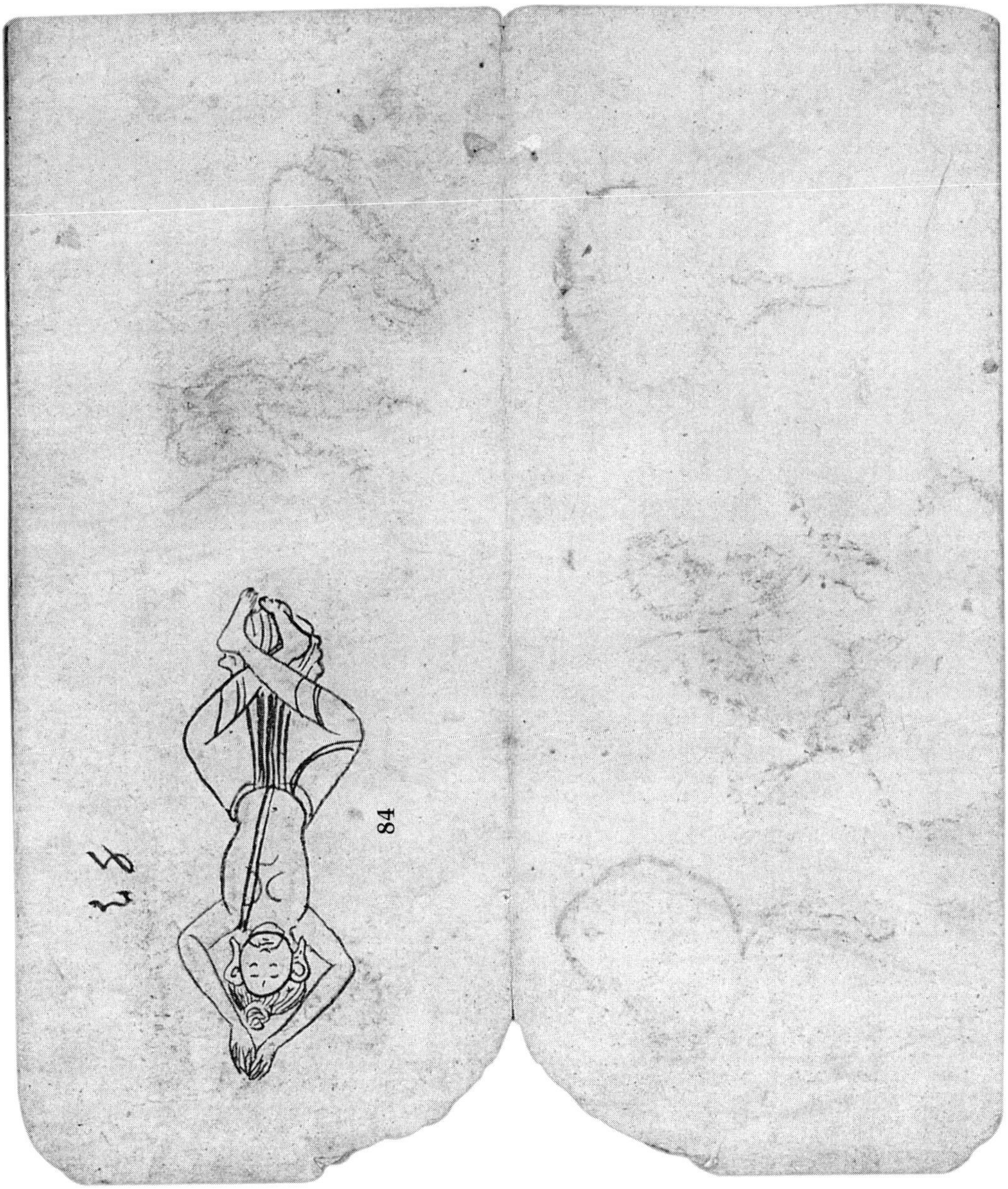

84

6.4 The Sources in the Jodhpur Tradition

6.4.1 A Description of the Line Drawings

A set of line drawings of the eighty-four Siddhas[77] performing eighty-four Yoga postures appears in two contemporary publications:

1) in the Appendix (pp. 1–21) of the book "Nava nātha caurāsī siddha" compiled by Yogin Naraharinātha and published by the Gorakṣanātha Maṭha (Vārāṇasī) in 1968; in the following I refer to it as N1; and

2) in the book titled "Nava nātha caurāsī siddha bālāsundarī yogamāyā" (pp. 3–23), published by Akhila Bhāratavarṣīya Yogapracāriṇī Mahāsabhā Prakāśanam (Puṇe) in 1968; I refer to this book as N2.

It appears that both books reproduced the drawings from a common source but added the names of the Siddhas separately, most likely using a list of names found in the original unidentified document. This explains the occurrence of some variants in the names between N1 and N2, although the drawings are identical. It is possible that the original document also listed the names of the *āsana*s which the Siddhas perform, but that these names were not copied by N1 and N2 because the two publications were primarily concerned with the eighty-four Siddhas.

The names of the Siddhas in this tradition are listed in table 2 as found in N1, after comparing them with two versions of the names printed in N2. One version of the names appears below the drawings, and another one as a separate list labelled 'The Eighty-four Siddhas Famous in Jodhpur, Rājasthān' on p. 26 of N2. Similar names are inscribed in a circa nineteenth-century painting from Jodhpur preserved in the Bhārat Kalā Bhavan, Vārāṇasī (no. 5362), and there labelled 'Maharaja Mansingh and Eighty-four Yogis.' The 'Yogis' in the painting are in fact the eighty-four Siddhas. It is not surprising that the Siddhas should be associated with Yogic postures, given that Matsyendra and his disciple Gorakṣa are traditionally considered the founders of *haṭhayoga*.

---

[77] Different Siddha traditions and lineages are described in Lokesh Chandra's "Dictionary of Buddhist Iconography" (volume 1, introduction pp. xii–xxv; see also volume 4: 1093–1096).

The names of the Siddhas in these sources belong to a tradition specific to Jodhpur and mostly differ from the names transmitted in other more well-known lineages. They are a mixture of Sanskrit and local forms, as can be seen from 28, where the suffix *pāva* is added to a Sanskrit name. This suffix is an honorific and stands for Sanskrit *pāda.*[78]

Lokesh Chandra reproduced the set of drawings from N1 in his "Dictionary of Buddhist Iconography,"[79] where he ascribes it to an "album published by Yogi Naraharinātha of Nepal for distribution to devotees." According to an inscription on the last page, the drawings are copies (*pratilipi*) of older drawings of the eighty-four Siddhas in the Jodhpur style. The copies were made by Prabhātnāth Yogī of the Division for the Propagation of Yoga (*yogapracāriṇī śākhā*) of the (Śrī) Siddha Ratnanāth Arts Institute (Kalā Kendra) at Caugharā in the Dāṅ district of western Nepal in 1968. The reputed Ratannāth Maṭha of the Gorakṣanātha sect is located at Caugharā.[80] The drawings are reproduced in section 6.4.2 from N1. Drawings 35 and 36 were printed upside down, an error I have corrected.

No information is provided about the original document from which the drawings were copied. However, the portraits of the Yogins in the line drawings are very similar to those of the eighty-four Siddhas painted on the walls of the sanctum of the large temple in Mahāmandir, just outside Jodhpur (section 6.4.3). The early-nineteenth-century murals and much later line drawings are clearly in the same tradition and may eventually be traceable to a common source.

Some of the Yoga postures depicted are similar to the ones described in Jayatarāma's Jogapradīpakā, which is not surprising since both documents are connected with traditions from Rājasthān. As is the case with the Nepalese set of illustrations, it is not possible to identify the *āsana*s without having access to a corresponding text.

For the eighty-four Siddhas/Mahāsiddhas, see Linrothe 2006. Dasgupta 1976: 202–210 also provides valuable information on Siddha traditions.

[78] For the suffix *pāva*, see Turner 1996: 454–455 (entry 8056). For some information on the suffixes *pā/phā*, see also Dasgupta 1976: 391, note 2. Dasgupta 1976: 392, note 3 lists the forms Kānupā/Kānuphā, Kāhnāi/Kānāi as dialectal variants of the Sanskrit name Kṛṣṇapāda.

[79] For these drawings, see volume 1, introduction, pp. xiv–xx.

[80] For more information on this Maṭha, see Unbescheid 1980: 18–25.

TABLE 2

The Names of the Eighty-four Siddhas in the Jodhpur Tradition
(following N1 and N2)

1) Ādikumārī
2) Kālāṅga
3) Gaurāṅga
4) Gorakṣa
5) Cauraṅgī
6) Carpaṭī
7) Śṛṅgī
8) Acala
9) Mīna
10) Matsyendra
11) Sajāī
12) Kapila
13) Kanthaḍi
14) Kaṇerī
15) Brahmananda
16) Govinda
17) Acaleśvara
18) Bālaguṇahāi
19) Vīravaṅka
20) Sārasvatāi
21) Sāgaragandha
22) Buddhāi
23) Bhūtāi
24) Kuṇḍalī
25) Kambalī
26) Maṇḍūkipāva[81]
27) Jālandhara
28) Śṛṅgāripāva[82]
29) Kānipāva
30) Naciketa
31) Vicāranātha
32) Dhūrmanātha
33) Vanakhaṇḍī
34) Hālipāva
35) Nandāi
36) Amarāi
37) Tanukubja
38) Agocara
39) Nāgārjuna
40) Sanaka
41) Sanandana
42) Satātana[83]
43) Sanatkumāra
44) Bhagnapātra
45) Dhāmaka
46) Dhūmaka
47) Khecara
48) Bhūcara
49) Śivagosvāmi[84]
50) Lohāṭīṭa[85]
51) Añjāipāva
52) Avaghaṭa

[81] The list in N2 reads Maṇḍukīpāva.

[82] The list in N2 reads Śṛṅgārīpāva.

[83] The list in N2 reads Sanātana.

[84] The list in N2 reads Śivagosvāmī.

[85] The list in N2 reads Lohāṭapaṭa.

53) Carmagosvāmī[86]
54) Gāvasiddha
55) Saurī
56) Bhramara
57) Canderī
58) Acalī
59) Viśaśaṃkhā[87]
60) Vilāpa
61) Milapā
62) Muktāi[88]
63) Pahūpanā
64) Cāla
65) Carmarāvala
66) Mālakī
67) Ghoḍācolī
68) Prakaṭīpāva
69) Lohā
70) Guṇiharṣa
71) Vāripāva
72) Ásthipāva
73) Sūtradaṇḍa
74) Lohapātra
75) Nāgeśa
76) Kulālipāva
77) Karpaṭī
78) Kanakāi
79) Himālaya
80) Tuṣakāi
81) Bālanātha
82) Mālākāra
83) Girivaranātha[89]
84) Rāmanātha

[86] N2 reads Carmagosvāmi. The list in N2 has two names, Carma and Gosvāmī.
[87] N2 reads Viśaṃkhā.
[88] The list in N2 reads Muktāī.
[89] The list in N2 omits this name.

6.4.2 A Reproduction of the Line Drawings

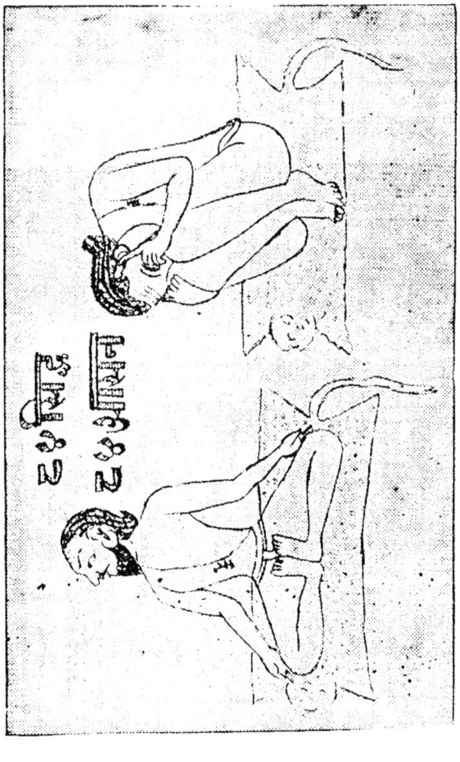

1 2

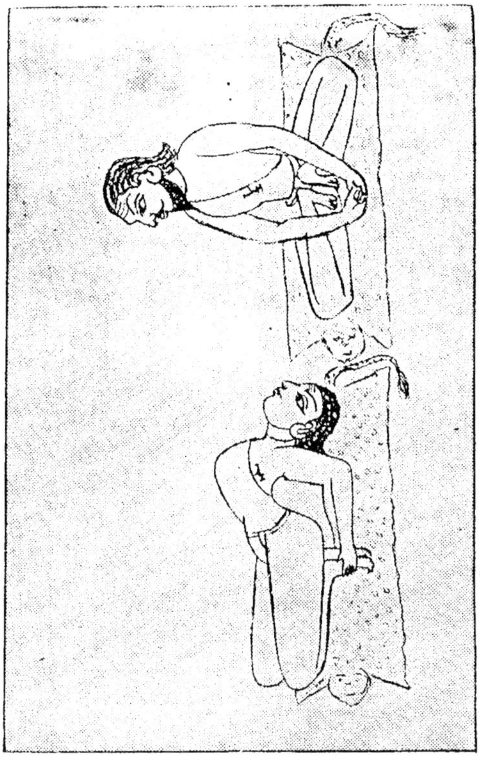

3 4

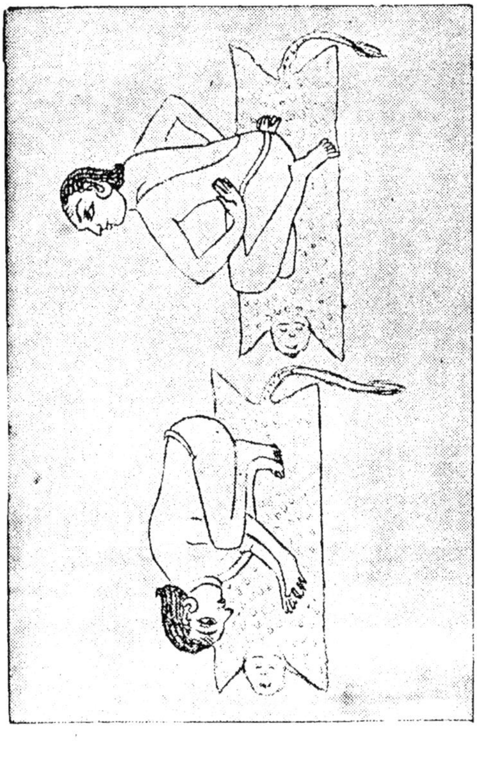

5 6

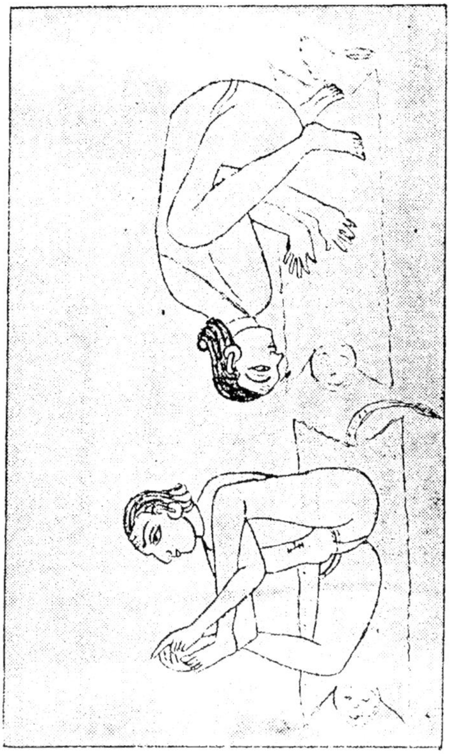

7 8

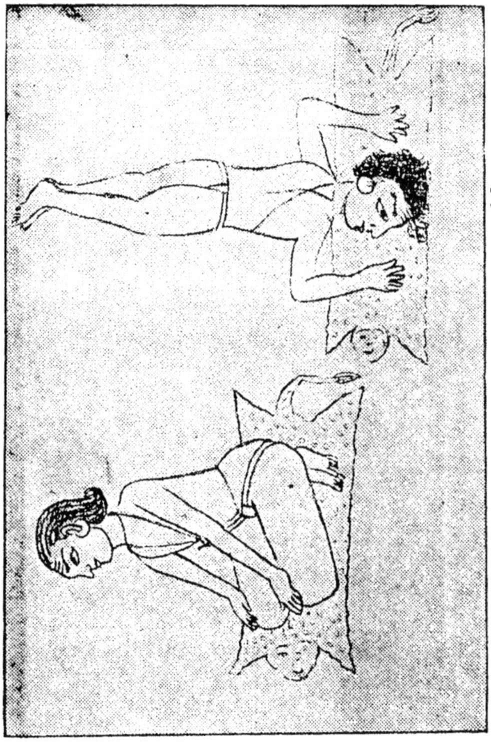

9 10

11 12

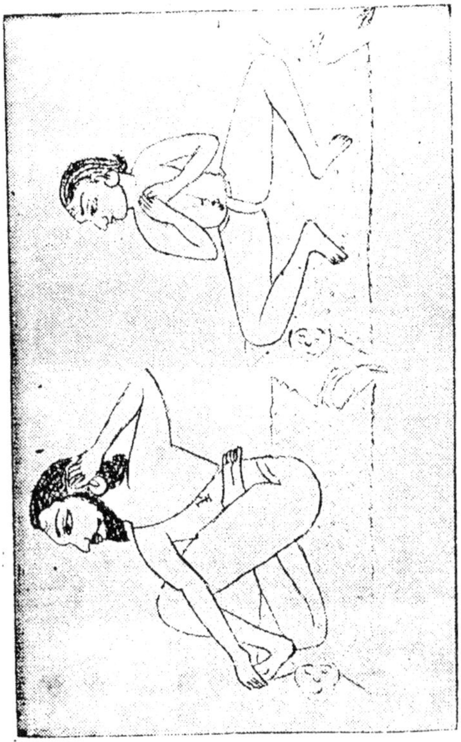

13 14

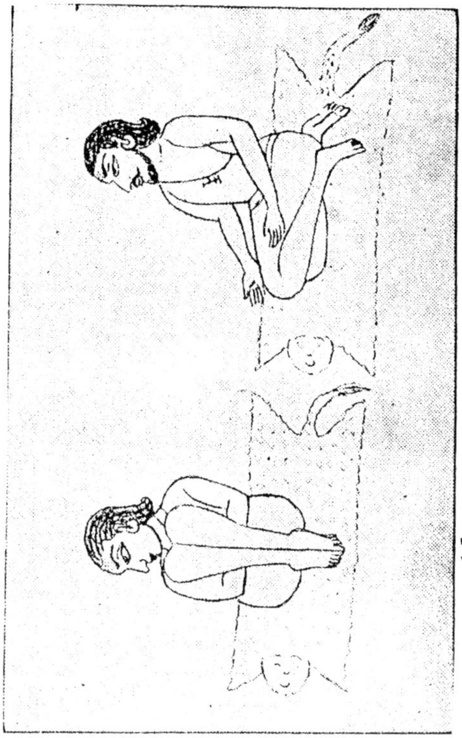

15 16

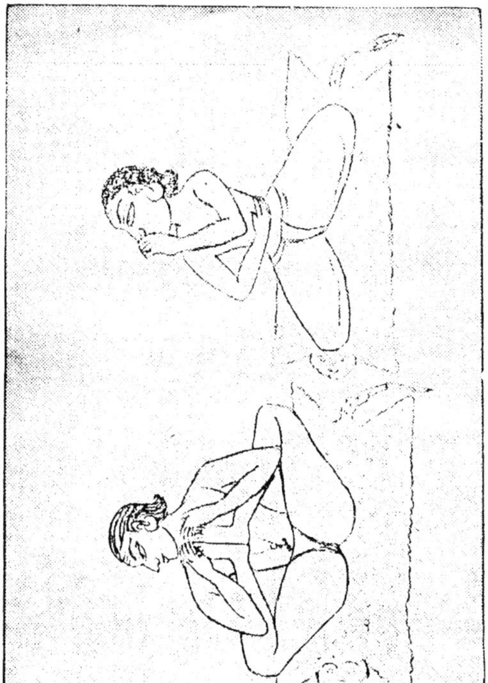

17 18

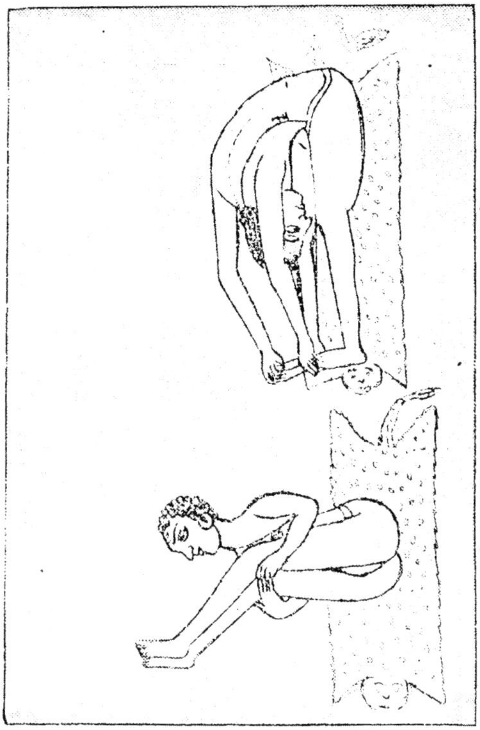

19 20

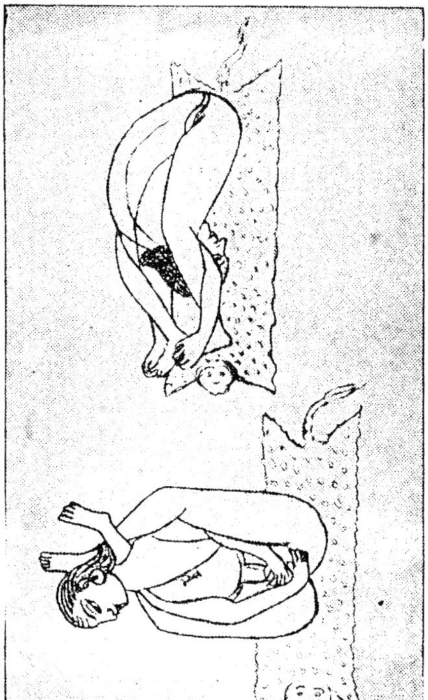

21 22

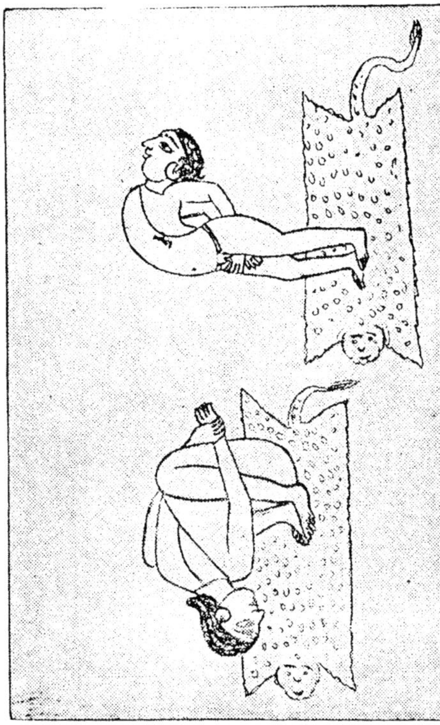

23 24

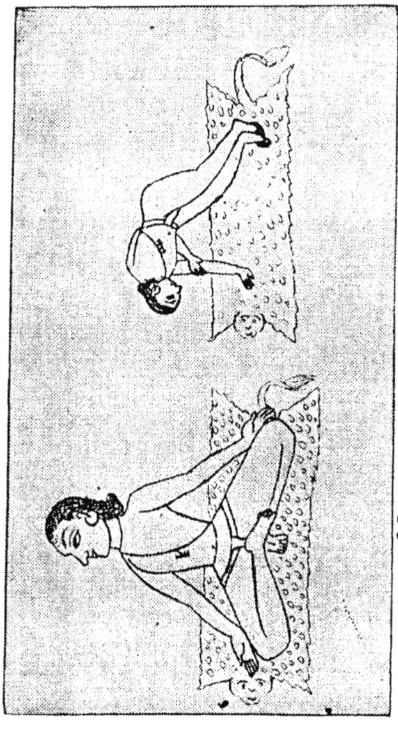

25 26

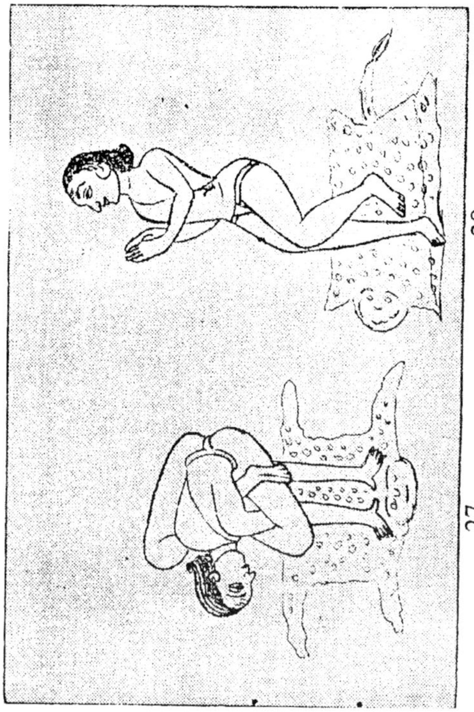

27 28

29 30

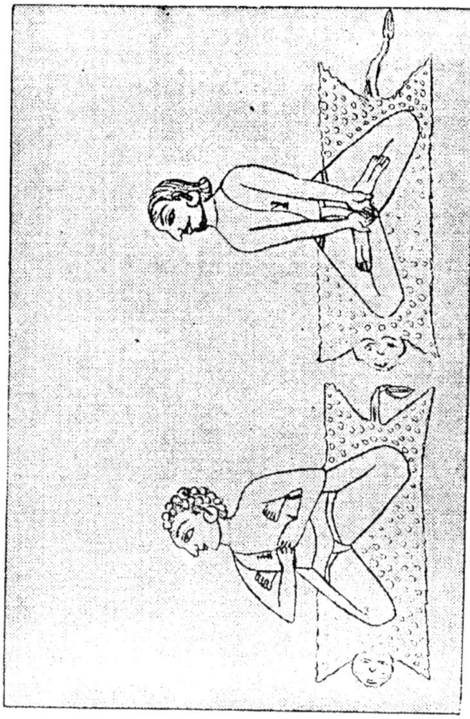

31 32

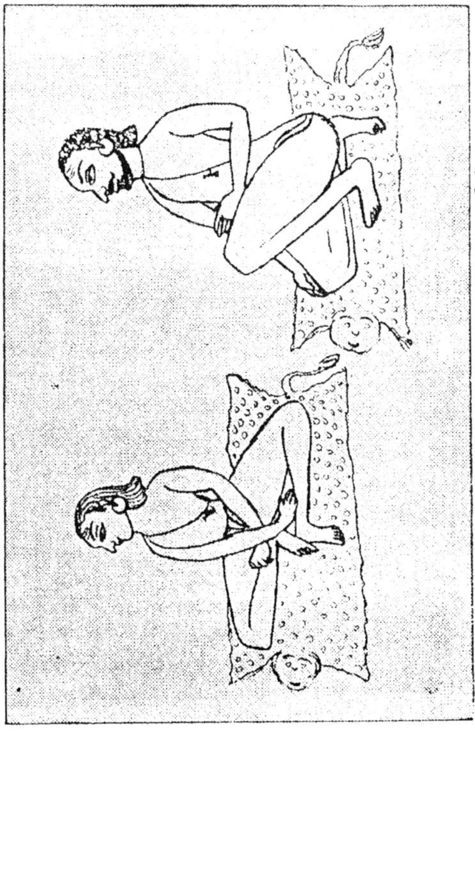

33 34

35 36

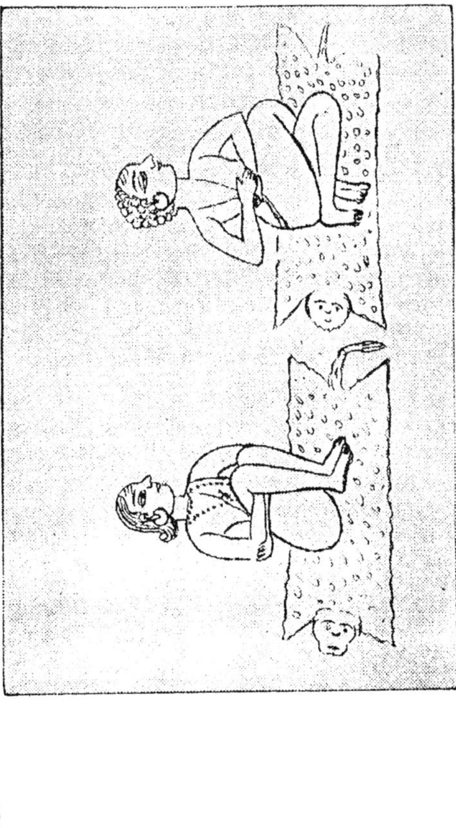

37 38

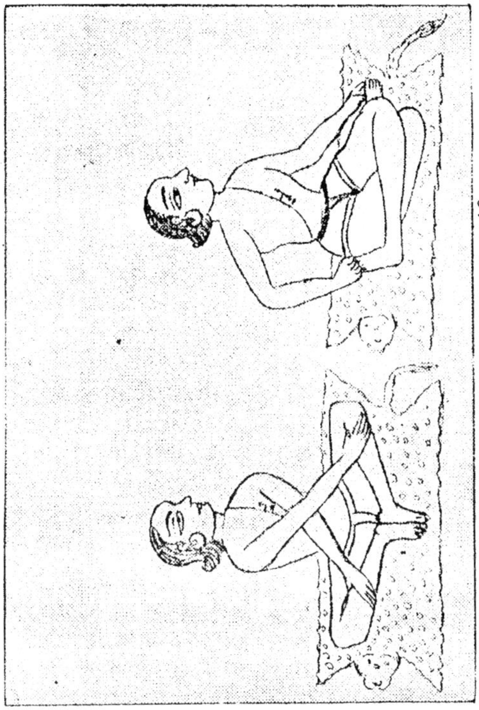

39 40

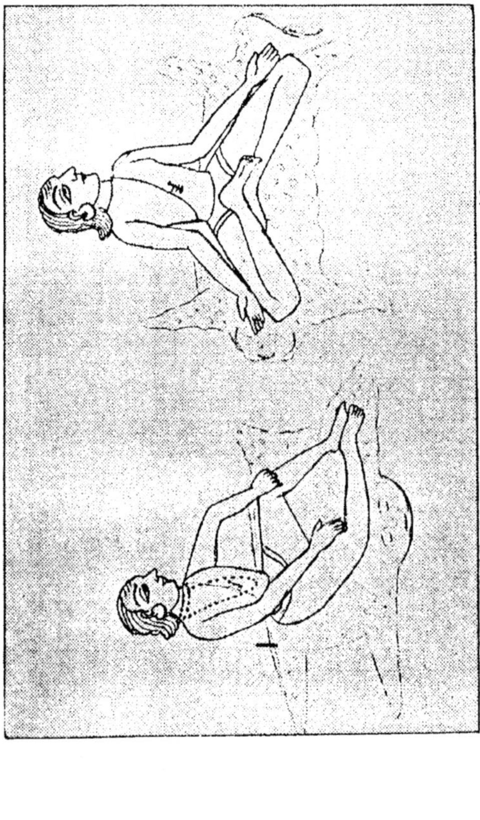

41 42

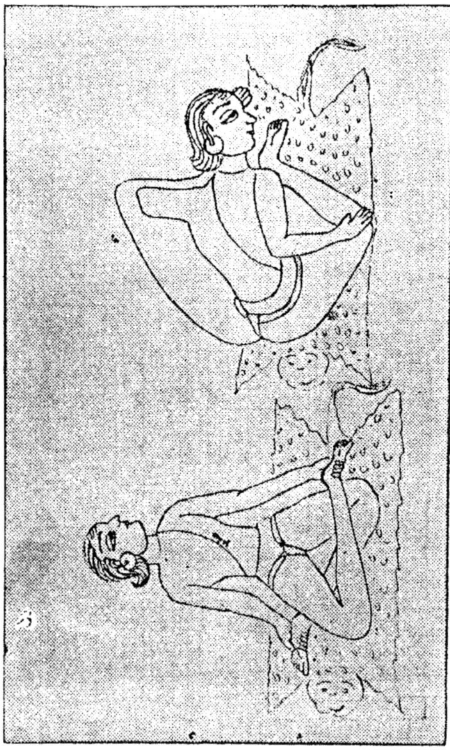

43 44

45 46

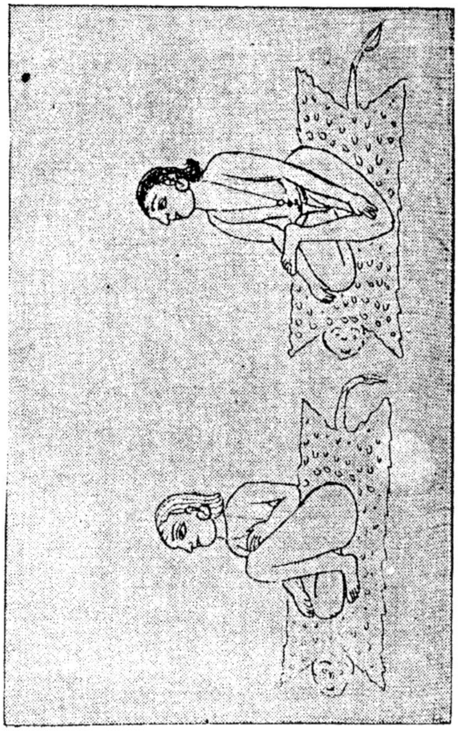

47 48

49

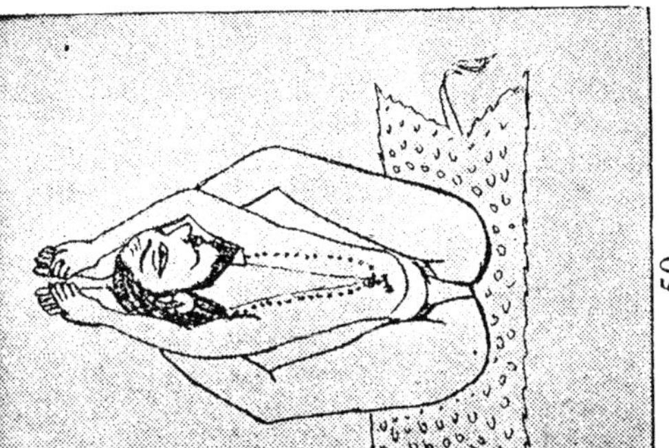

50

51

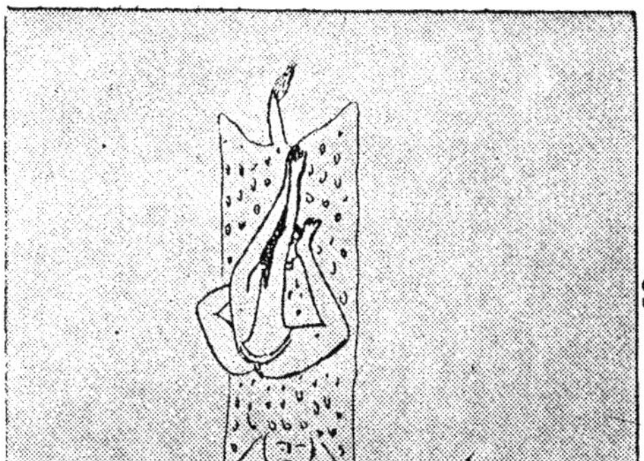

52

53

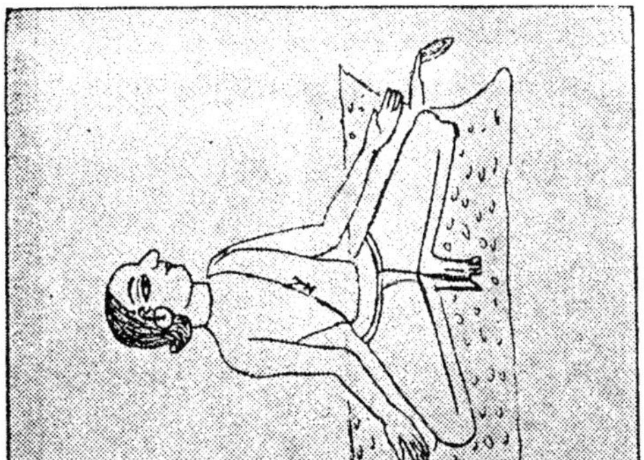

54

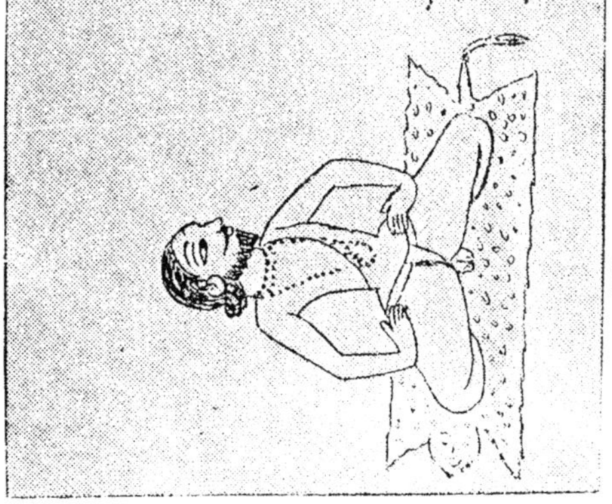

55

56

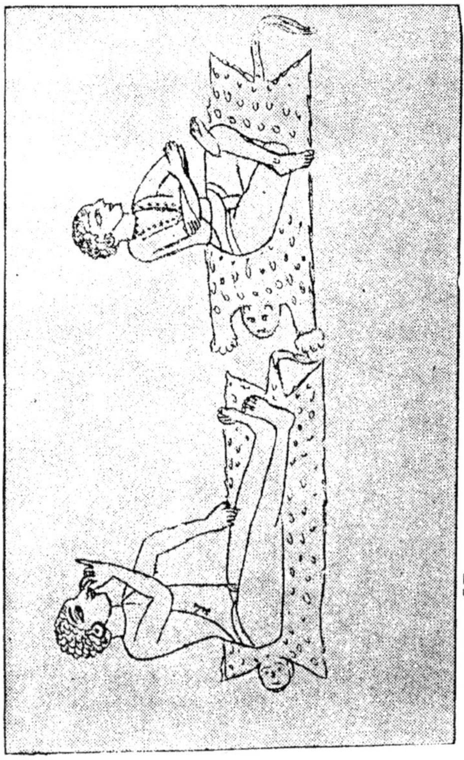

57 58

59 60

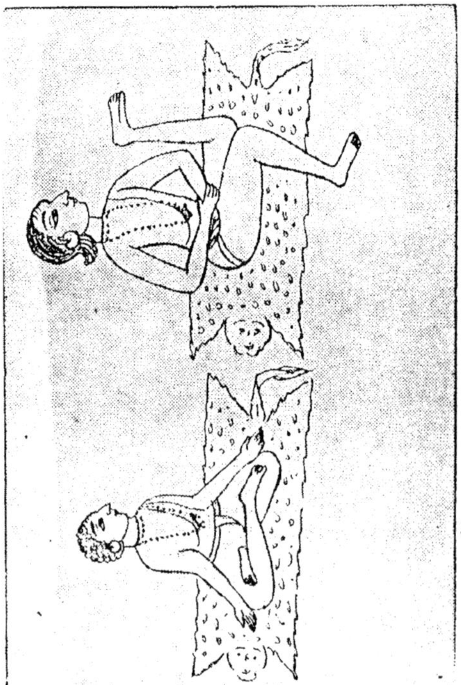

61 62

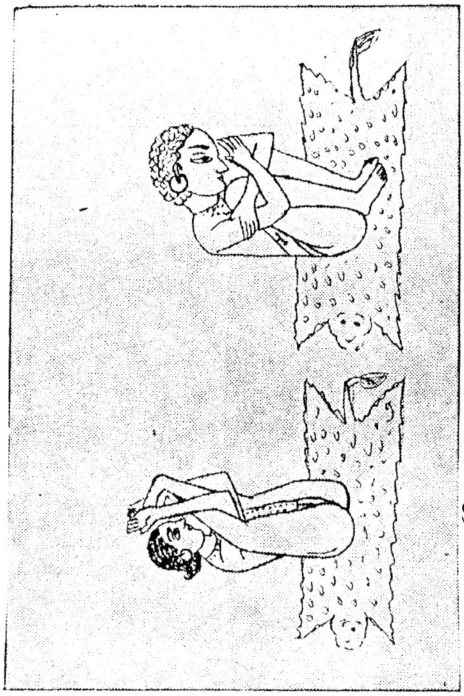

63 64

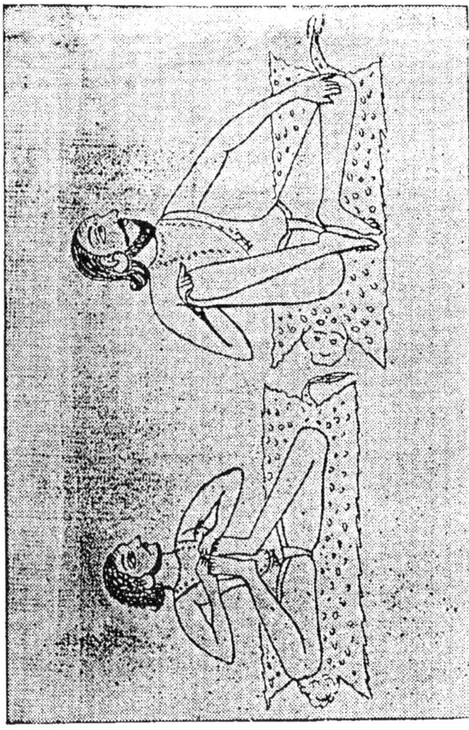

65 66

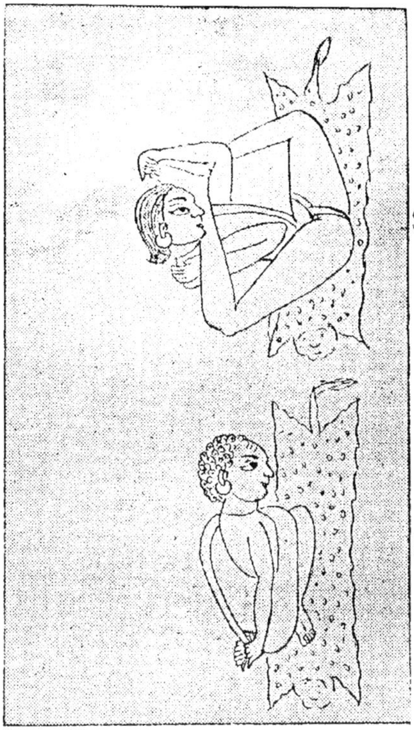

67 68

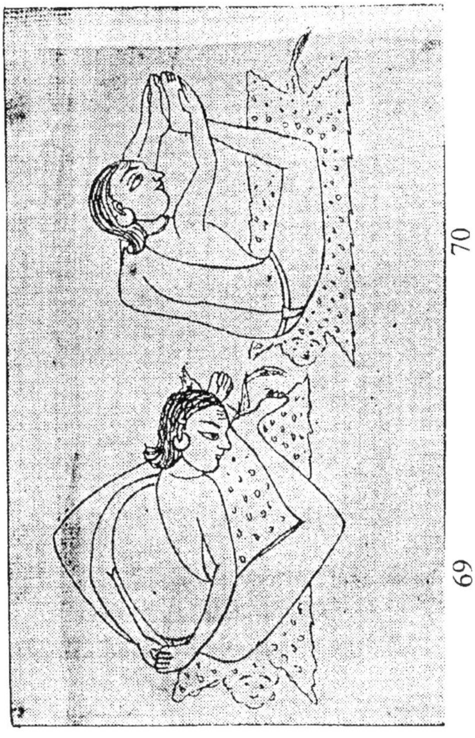

69 70

71 72

73 74

75 76

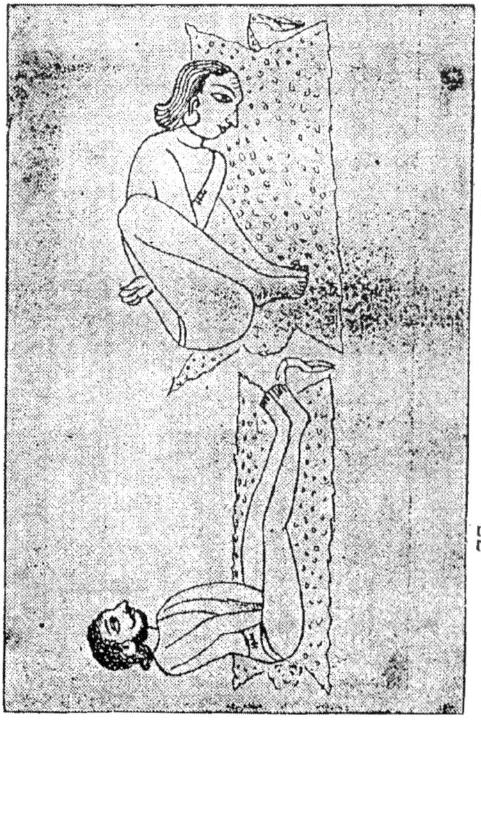

77 78

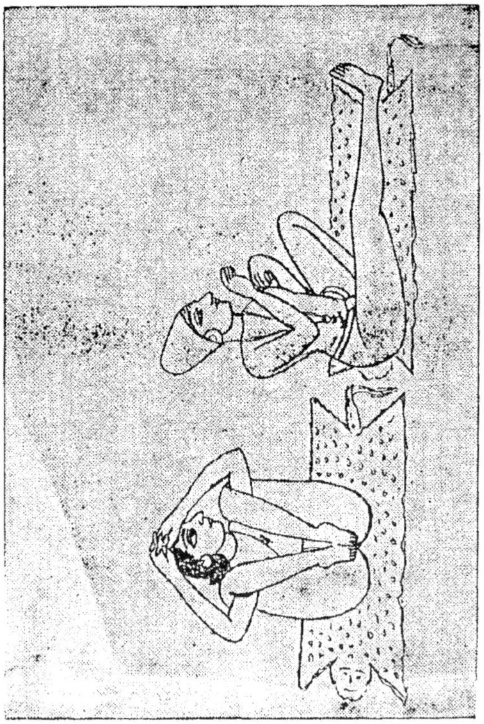

79 80

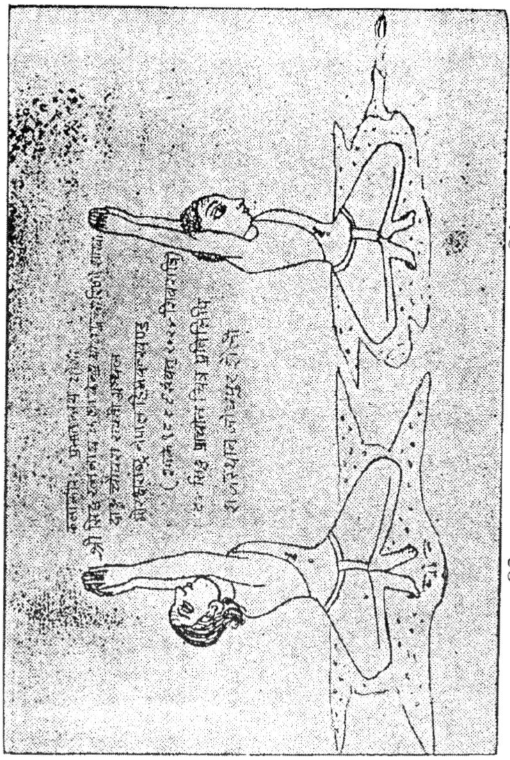

83 84

81 82

6.4.3 The Murals in Mahāmandir

Portraits of the eighty-four Siddhas performing different *āsanas* decorate the walls of the sanctum of the large temple at the Mahāmandir temple complex just outside Jodhpur, in central Rājasthān. The construction of this Nātha temple was completed under Mān Singh, the Mahārāja of Marwar, in 1805. The murals possibly date from 1810. Unlike the line drawings discussed in section 6.4.1, which are very similar, these murals are not labelled. A particular sequence of practitioners is hard to determine since the portraits of the Siddhas are painted in a continuous register across the walls, without framed divisions between them. Most Siddhas wear the large earrings typical of the *kānphaṭa* Yogins. Each Siddha is seen in his own hut performing a different but unidentified *āsana*. We do not know anything about the sources the artist used for painting the postures. Perhaps he had a set of drawings or paintings at his disposal, which may still be stored in some Jodhpur collection. The basis for the line drawings must have been some source within the same tradition. That source must have also contained the Siddhas' names, and perhaps, too, the names of the *āsanas* they are performing.

Murals similar to the ones in Mahāmandir that show the eighty-four Siddhas performing *āsanas* are also found on the walls of the sanctum of Udaimandir in Jodhpur. The temple was constructed under Mān Singh in 1821. The paintings are of inferior quality and the postures often mirror images of the ones in Mahāmandir.

The complete set of the portraits of the individual Siddhas in Mahāmandir has not been published. One portrait photographed by D. White is reproduced on a book cover (White 1996) and three portraits are reproduced in Linrothe 2006: 413. In this book I reproduce photographs of sixteeen individual portraits. They correspond to line drawings 1, 4, 11, 21, 25, 32, 34, 46, 50, 53, 58, 60, 64, 65, 68 and 71. The photographs were taken by R. Linrothe who kindly made them available for publication in this book.

6.4.4 A Reproduction of Selected Murals
(Photographs courtesy of Rob Linrothe)

1

4

11

21

25

32

34

46

50

53

58

60

64

65

68

71

6.5 The Line Drawings in Svāmī Svayamānanda 1992

1

2

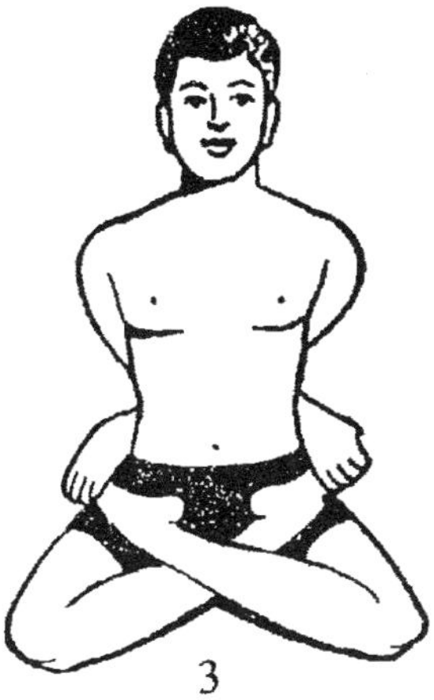

3

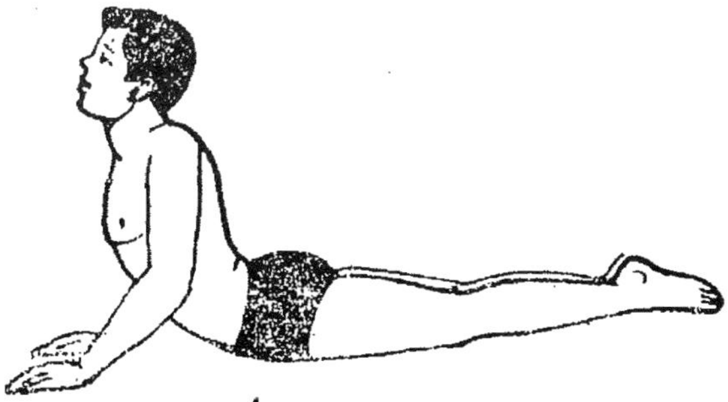

4

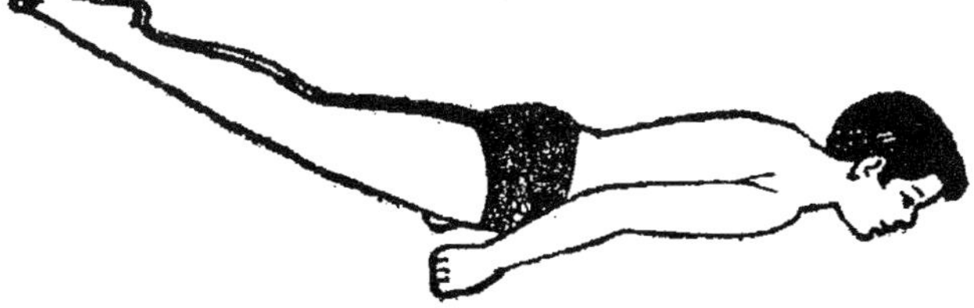

5

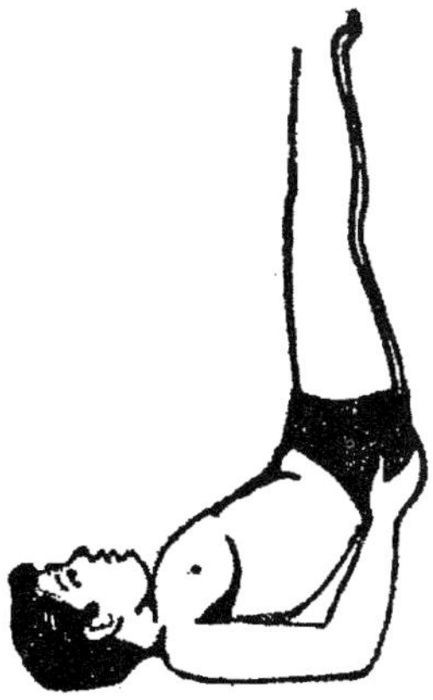

6

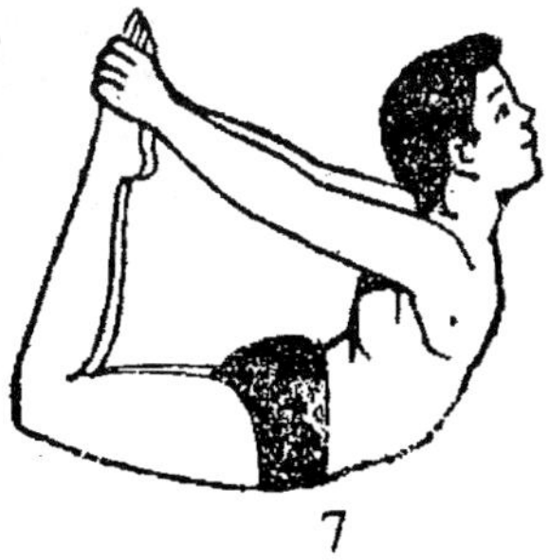

7

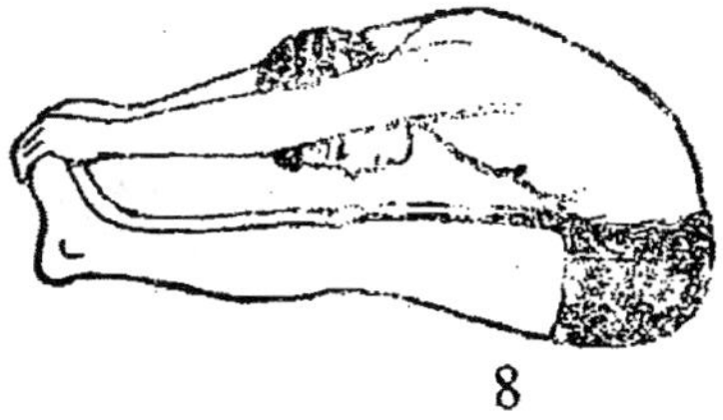

8

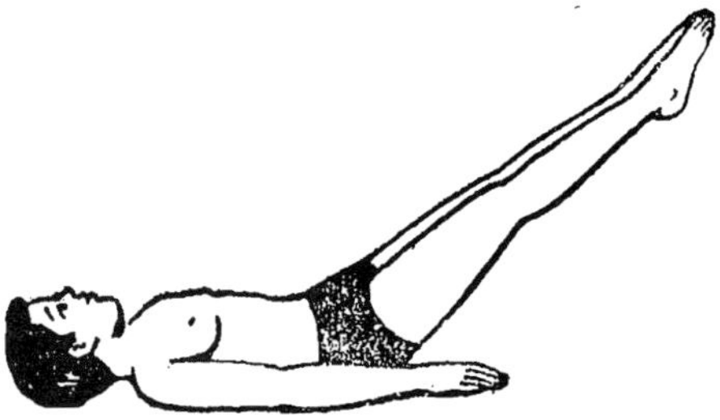

10

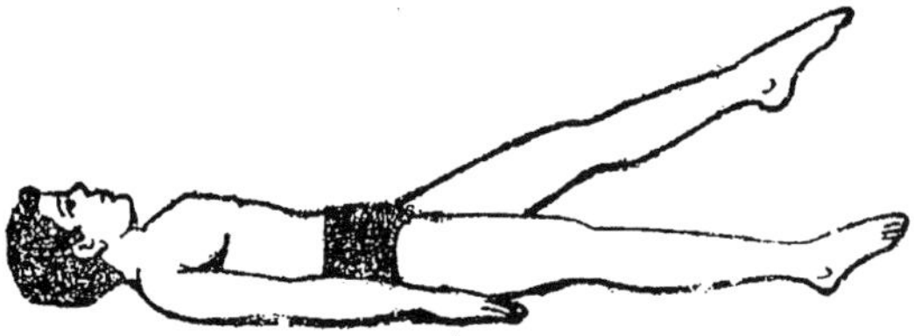

11

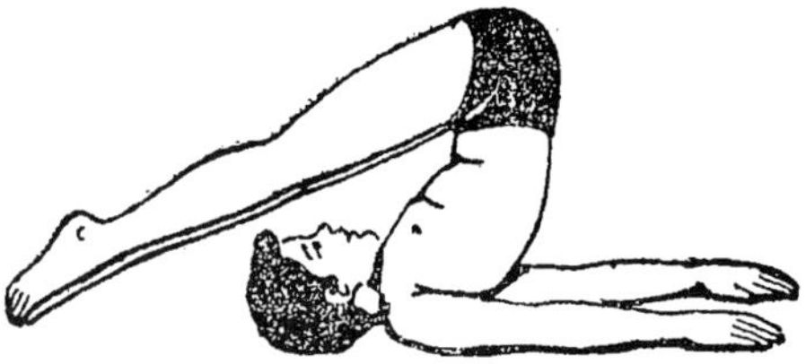

12

13

14

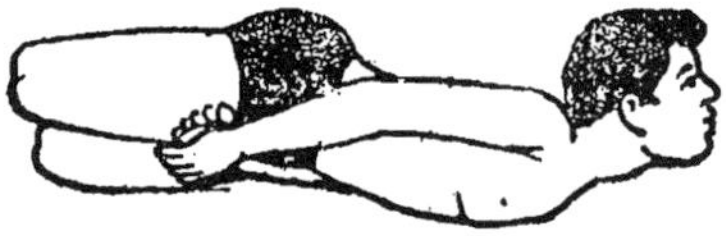

16

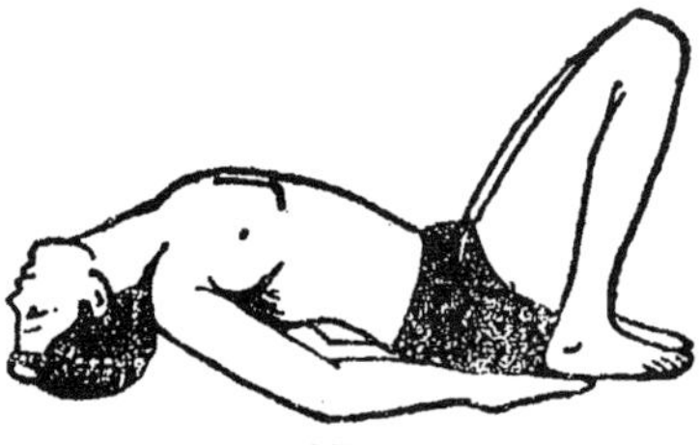

17

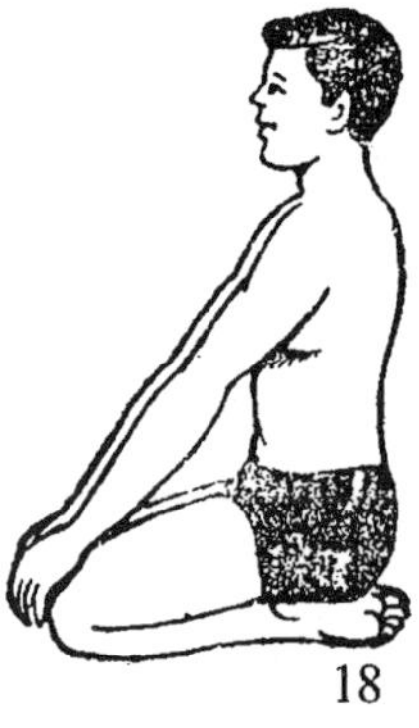

18

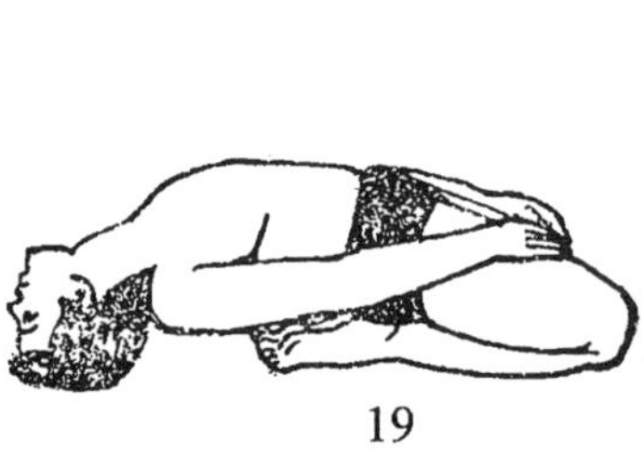

19

20

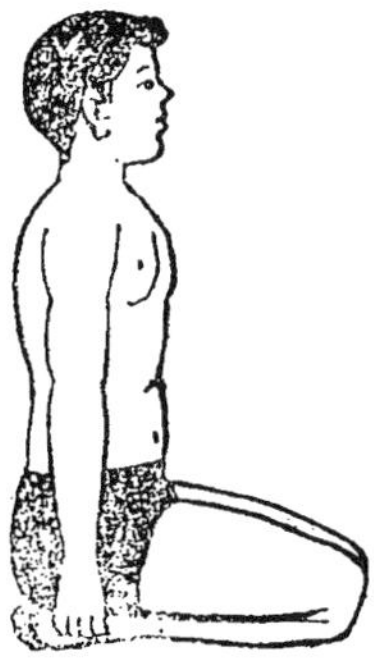

21

23

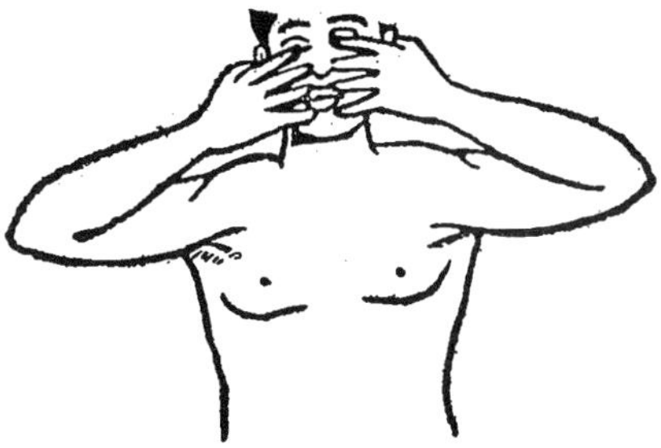

24

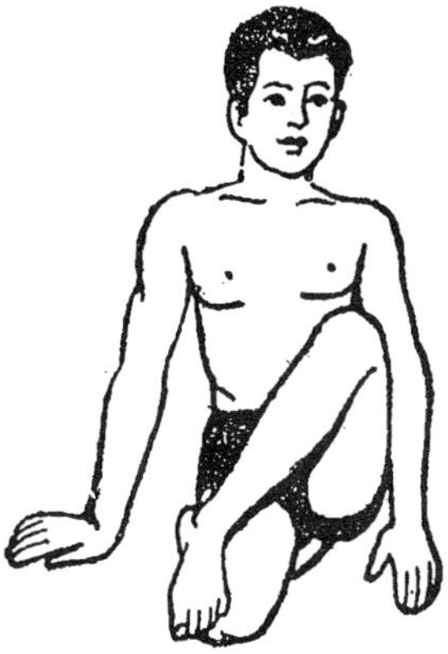

25

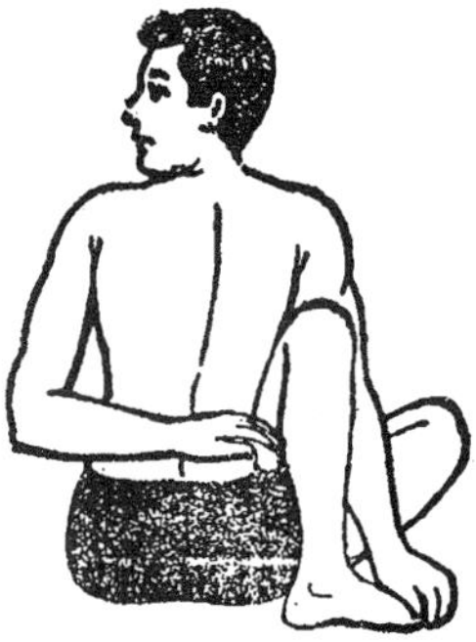

26

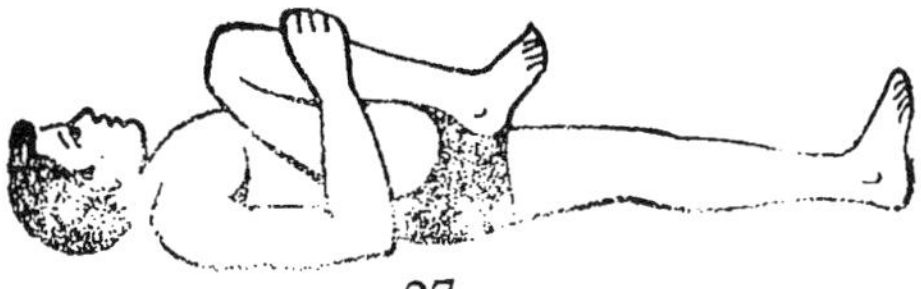

27

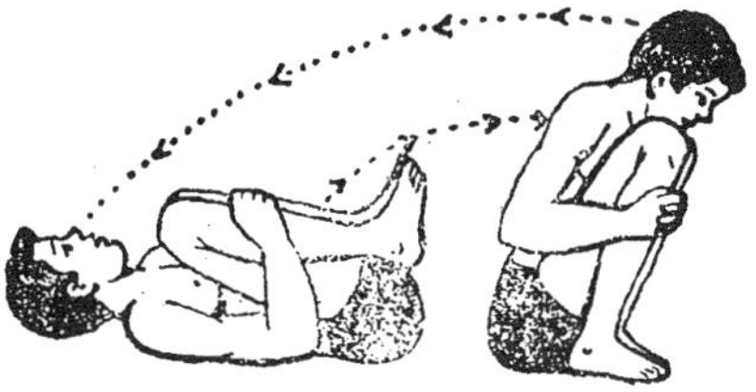

28

29

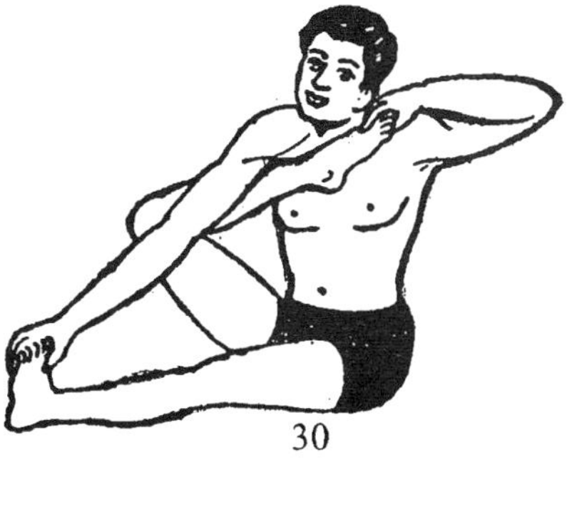

30

31

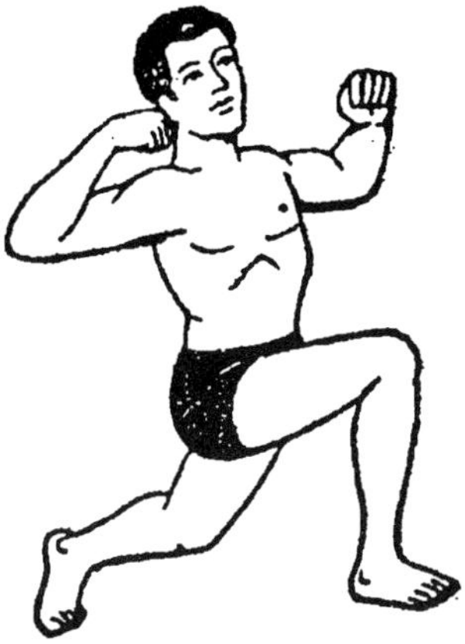

32

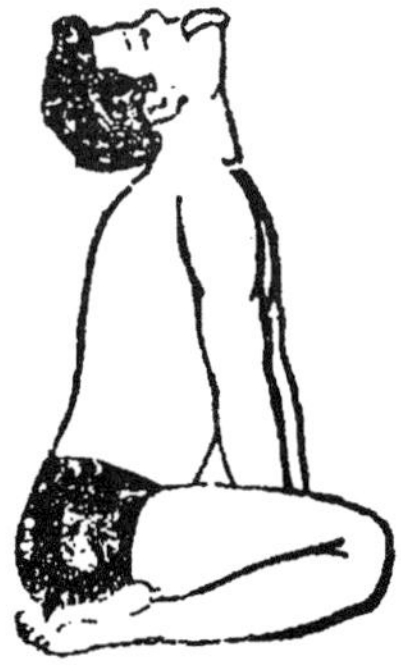

33

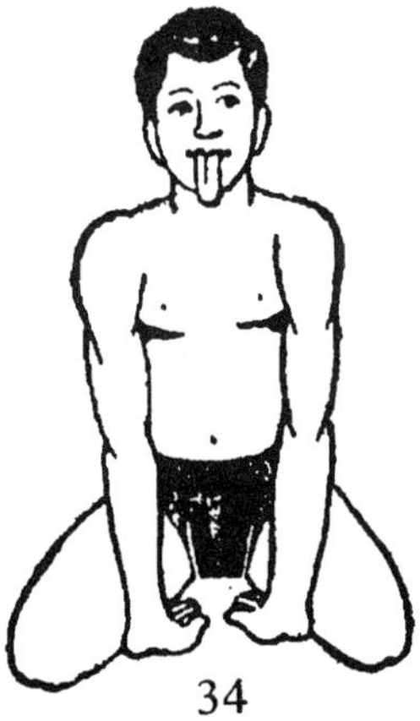

34

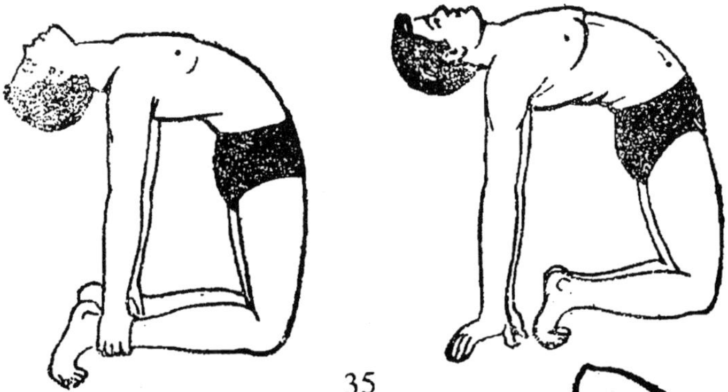

35

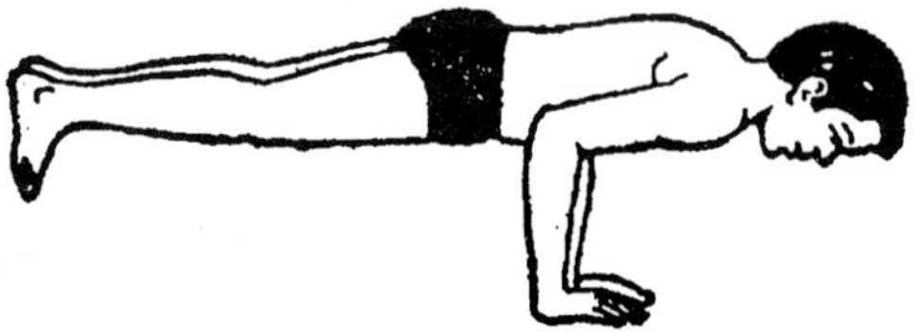

36

37

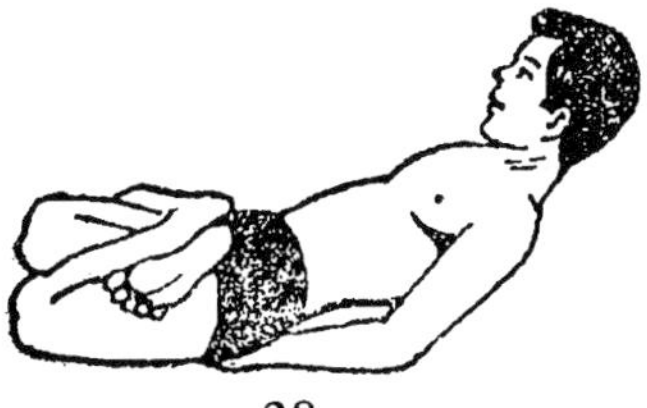

38

39

40

41

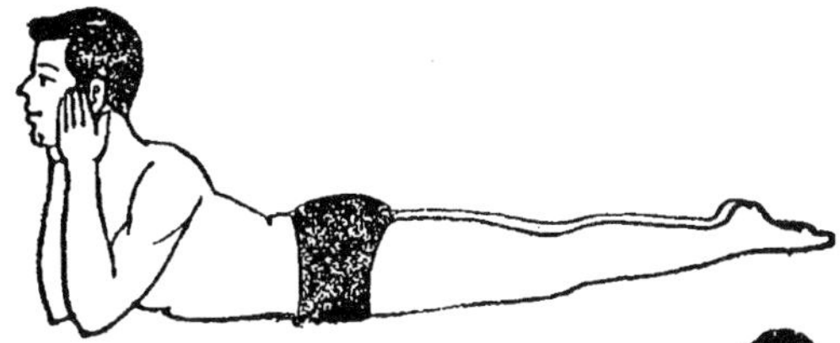

42

43

44

45

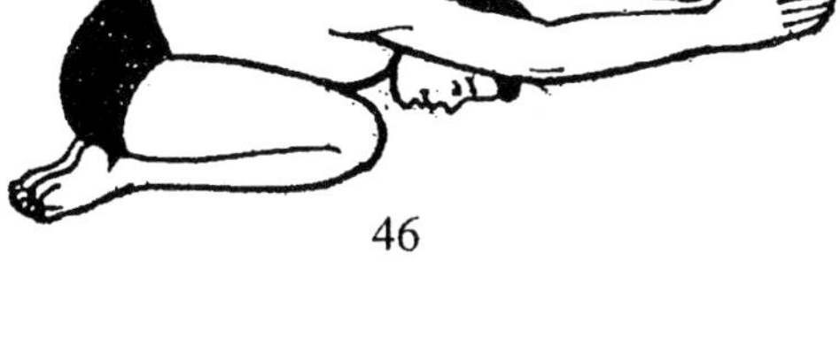

46

47

48

49

50

51

52

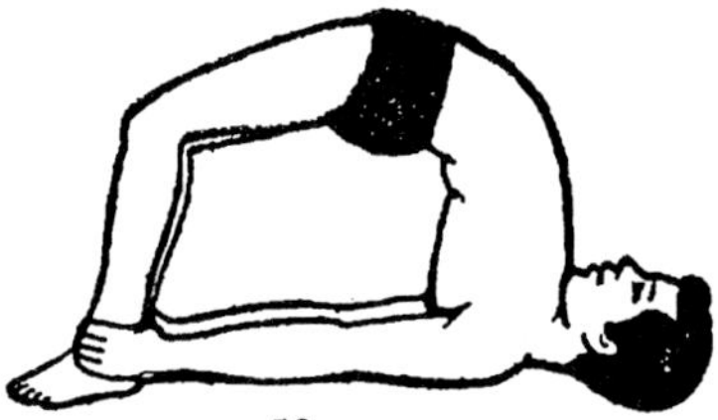

53

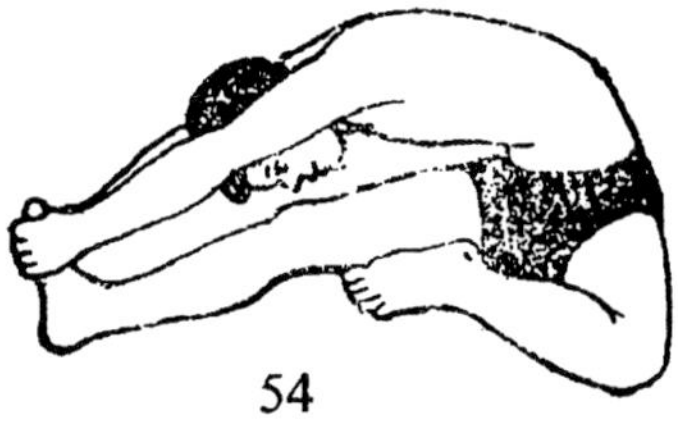

54

55

56

57

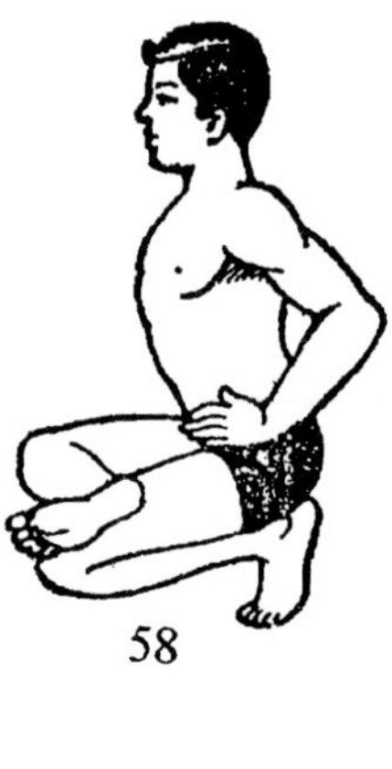

58

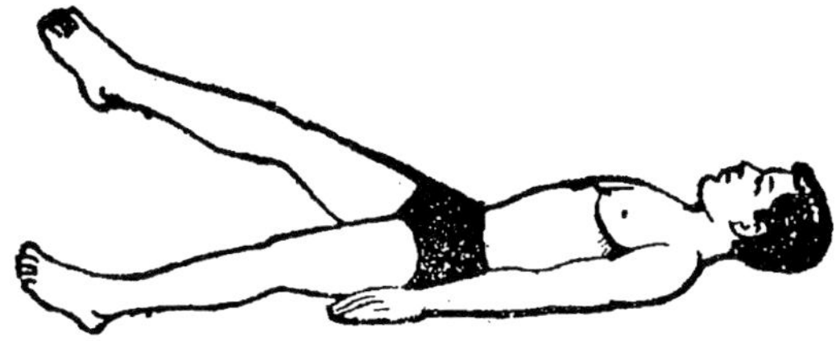
59

60

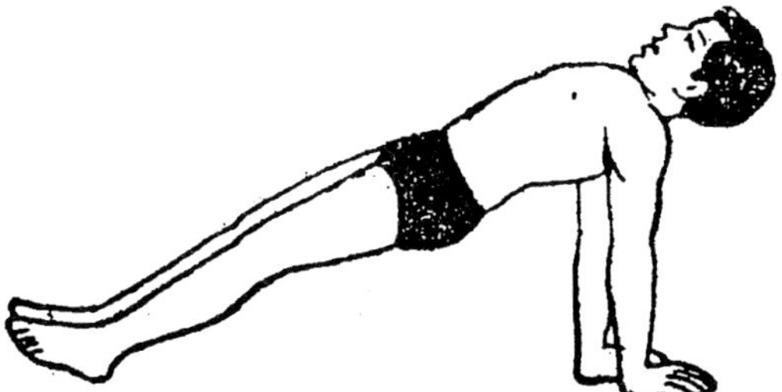
61

62

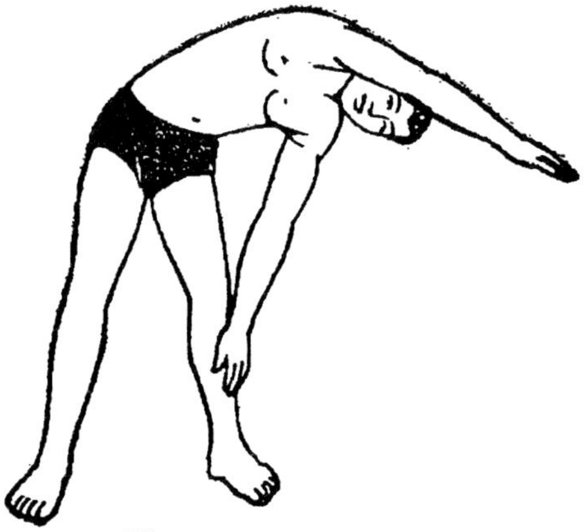
63

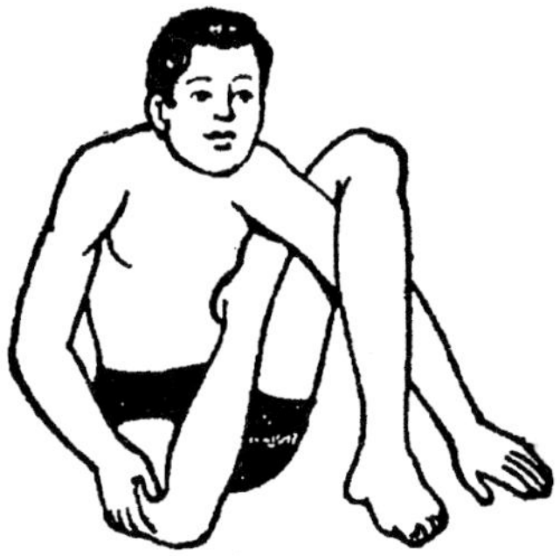
64

65

66

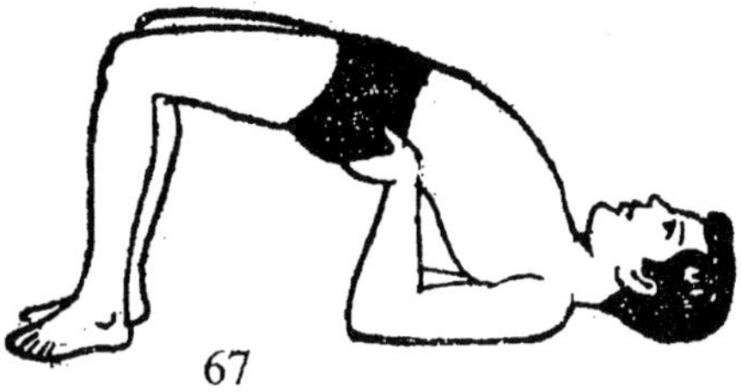

67

68

69

70

71

72

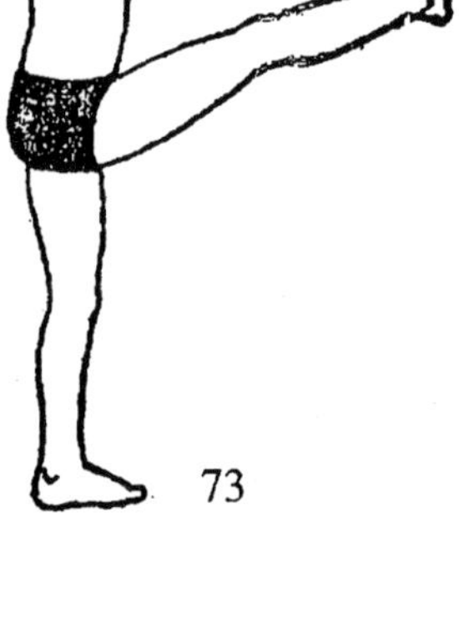

73

74

75

76

77

78

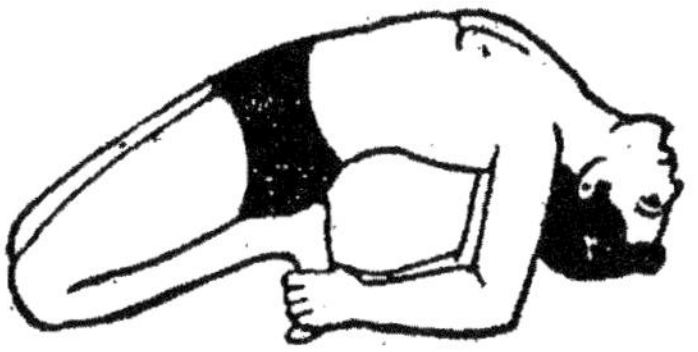
79

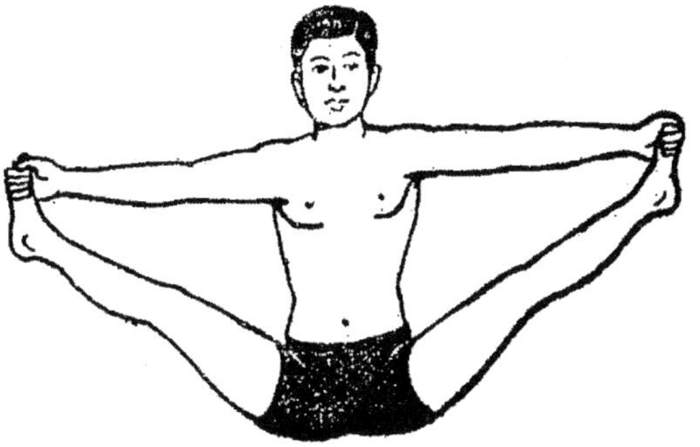
80

81

82

83

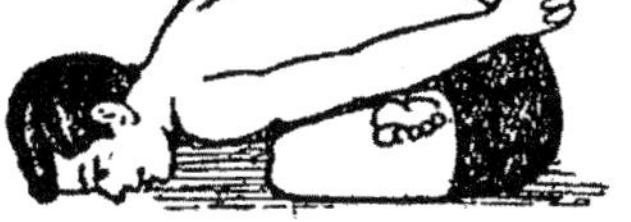
84

6.6 Photographs of the Āsanas in the Yoga Challenge® System

1.1

1.2

1.3

2.1

2.2

2.3

2.4

2.5

2.6

2.7

2.8

2.9

2.10

2.11

2.12

2.13

2.14

2.15

2.16

2.17

2.18

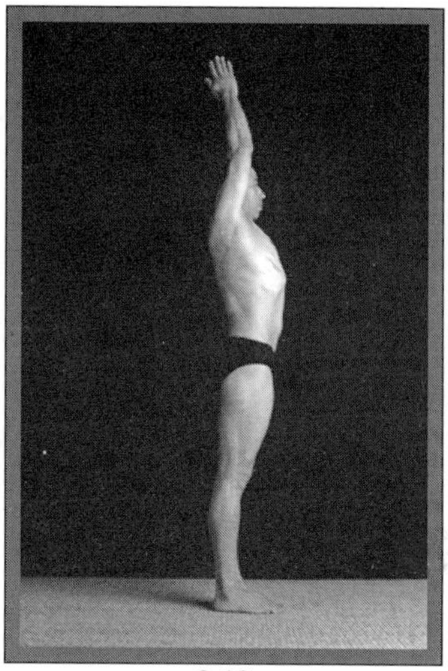
2.19

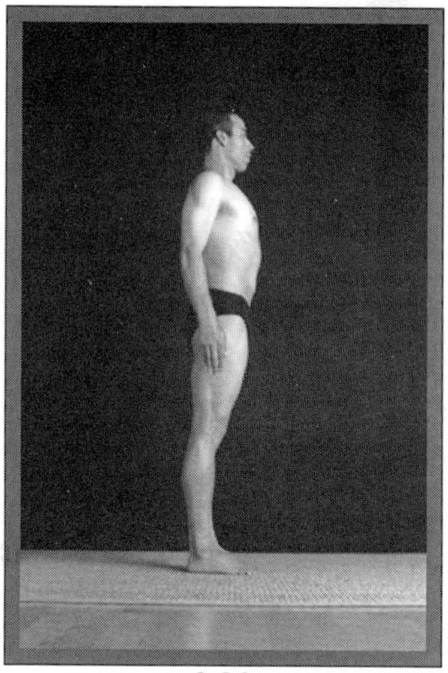
2.20

3.1

3.2

4

5

6

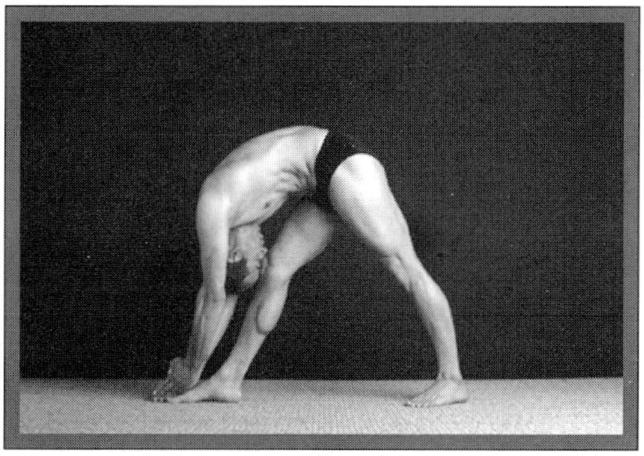
7

8.1

8.2

8.3

9

10

11

12

13

14

15

16

17

18

19

20

21

22

23

24

25

26

27

28

29

30

31

32

33

34

35

36

37

38.1

38.2

39

40.1

40.2

41

42

43

44

45

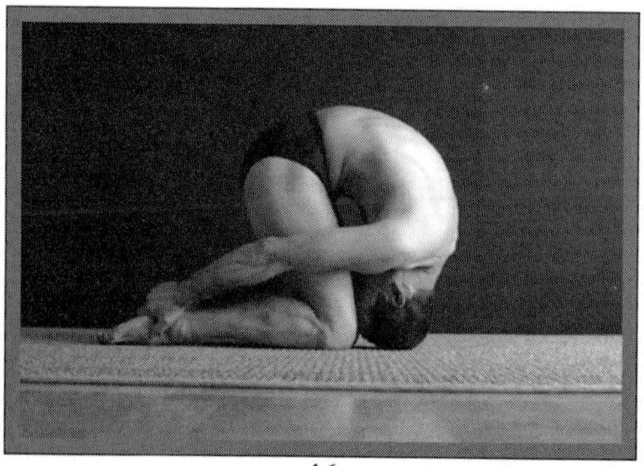
46

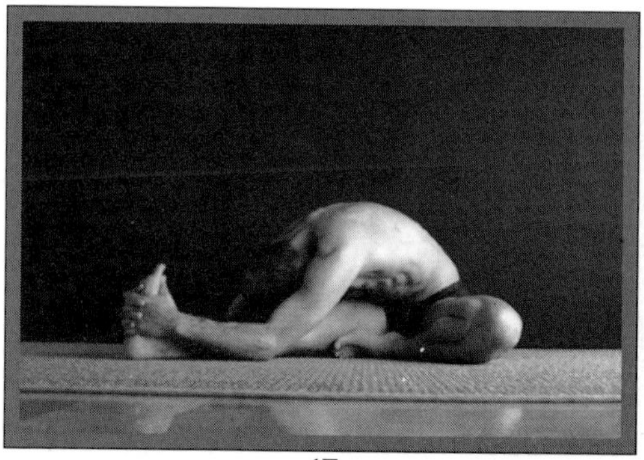
47

48

49

50

51

52

53

54

55

56

57

58

59

60

61

62

63

64

65

66

67

68

69

70

71

72

73

74

75

76

77

78

79

80

81

82

83

84

7. Concluding Remarks

As I have shown in section 4.2, *āsanas* feature among the ancillary parts (*aṅga*) of many traditional Yoga systems but occupy a subordinate position. Authorities usually viewed them as a prerequisite for meditation (*dhyāna*). Postures gained more importance in the later Nātha tradition, where they became associated with practices usually subsumed under the term *haṭhayoga*. This is a somewhat fuzzy term which is interpreted differently by authors, as I have discussed in section 3. In texts of the Nātha tradition, we find a larger number of postures described, some of which are taught for strengthening the body and stabilizing it. But even in this tradition *āsanas* were not the main focus of practice. Moreover, their performance was usually combined with that of 'energy locks' (*bandha*) and control of the breath. The exclusive practice of *āsanas* for gaining physical strength and health and their inclusion within athletic routines is the result of a relatively modern development fostered by physical culturists, who have expanded the number of postures by adding new ones and variations on the old ones. Despite frequently made claims, those modern Yoga schools which exclusively focus on postures represent neither the teachings of the Yogasūtra nor those of the Nātha tradition.

Practitioners often assert that their postures are derived from an ancient tradition of eighty-four classical *āsanas*. The main goal of this book has been to trace and document such tradition(s) in Yoga. Although some texts refer to 84,000 postures said to have been condensed into eighty-four postures, this many postures are rarely described in older texts. However, contrary to a statement made by Shashibhusan Dasgupta (1976: 205) that eighty-four *āsanas* are not described anywhere, several lists of names of eighty-four *āsanas* could be located, although all of them are comparatively late.

The oldest list of names of eighty-four *āsanas* appears in the seventeenth-century Haṭharatnāvalī, a Sanskrit text by Śrīnivāsa from Āndhra, South India. The oldest text which provides a list of names as well as descriptions of eighty-four postures is the eighteenth-century Jogapradīpakā by Jayatarāma from North India, written in a mixed Hindī. (A set of coloured drawings from the nineteenth century illustrating the *āsana*s according to the descriptions in the Jogapradīpakā is reproduced in this book.) The lists of eighty-four *āsana*s in the Haṭharatnāvalī and the Jogapradīpakā are entirely different. They also differ from descriptions of eighty-four *āsana*s which I found in four contemporary publications. Thus all of the six lists I examined are at variance, except list 8.3. This list is found in two modern books, Daniélou 1949 and Haṇmaṃte 1980, both of which are based on an article by Śarmā published in 1935. Many *āsana* names are only found in a single list. Only the lotus posture (Padmāsana), peacock posture (Mayūrāsana) and Siddhāsana (including the variant Siddhi/Siddha āsana in list 8.2) appear in all six lists. Two of these postures, Padmāsana and Siddhāsana, are ancient and important postures for meditation. In some of the lists we encounter uncommon names, which are not recorded elsewhere. However, since the names of *āsana*s often vary in different traditions not many conclusions can be drawn from mere lists of names of eighty-four postures without descriptions of them. Whatever their histories may be, the lists of names were certainly independently transmitted and cannot be traced to one single original list. None of the lists of names of eighty-four *āsana*s gathered in this book goes far back in time. Thus we do not have access to an ancient tradition of eighty-four *āsana*s, or to a tradition from which modern *āsana* systems can be derived. There is also no evidence that such a tradition ever existed.

Eighty-four and 84,000 are mystical numbers traditionally indicating completeness and sometimes sacredness. Most influential for the Yoga tradition of eighty-four postures must have been the tradition of eighty-four Mahāsiddhas, whose names are recorded in a number of lists, in which they vary considerably. The eighty-four Siddhas are frequently represented in art, occasionally as having assumed Yogic postures. The number eighty-four has continued to be influential up to modern times in circles of Yoga practitioners. Because of its symbolic significance and because ancient lists of eighty-four *āsana*s are not easily accessible, several modern Yoga teachers have taken to compiling their own lists of postures. Honouring the number eighty-four, they included postures they considered to be important, but every teacher has included different postures and combined them into different sequences in his/her list. In the course of my research I came across several such lists which identify themselves as modern compilations by Western authors from books written by contemporary Yoga teachers. They have been excluded from this study. In their motivations for compiling lists of eighty-four postures, however, the modern practitioners may not differ from the authors of the older texts Haṭharatnāvalī and the Jogapradīpakā, who themselves may have likewise compiled their lists. Otherwise one wonders why these two texts provide no information about the lineages through which the *āsana* lists were transmitted. In this way, ancient and modern teachers appear to have developed their own systems of *āsanas* acknowledging the number eighty-four.

8. Appendices: Lists of Names of Eighty-four Āsanas[90]

8.1 Haṭharatnāvalī 3.9–20[91]

1) Siddhāsana
2) Bhadrāsana
3) Vajrāsana
4) Siṃhāsana
5) Śilpāsana[92]
6) Bandhapadmāsana[93]
7) Karapadmāsana
8) Samputitapadmāsana
9) Śuddhapadmāsana
10) Daṇḍamayūrāsana
11) Pārśvamayūrāsana
12) Sahajamayūrāsana
13) Bandhamayūrāsana[94]
14) Piṇḍamayūrāsana
15) Ekapādamayūrāsana
16) Bhairavāsana
17) Kāmadahanāsana
18) Pāṇipātrāsana
19) Kārmukāsana[95]
20) Svastikāsana

---

[90] In the Appendices I have standardized the orthography of the names to a certain extent. I have, for example, removed hyphens in the names of *āsanas* except for cases where the Sanskrit vowel *sandhi* (that is, the coming together of two vowels) was not observed.
[91] I mostly follow the text of the edition HR2 3.9–20, in which the names of the postures differ occasionally from those listed in the older edition HR1 3.8–19. In addition, I have taken versions of the names of the postures described in HR2 3.25–76 into consideration. I have added the word *āsana* to many names, unless the synonym *pīṭha* was used or a name ended in *mudrā*. The text of the HR often omits the word *āsana* because of metrical constraints.
[92] HR1 reads Śilpasiṃhāsana.
[93] HR1, combining 6 and 7, reads Bandhakara.
[94] HR2 3.45d gives the synonym Baddhakekī with the variant reading Bandhakekī.

21) Gomukhāsana

22) Vīrāsana

23) Maṇḍūkāsana

24) Markaṭāsana

25) Matsyendrāsana

26) Pārśvamatsyendrāsana

27) Bandhamatsyendrāsana[96]

28) Nirālambanāsana

29) Cāndrāsana

30) Kāṇṭhavāsana[97]

31) Ekapādāsana

32) Phaṇīndrāsana

33) Paścimatānāsana

34) Śayitapaścimatānāsana

35) <Vi>citrakaraṇī[98] <mudrā>

36) Yoganidrā[99] <mudrā>

37) Vidhūnanāsana[100]

38) Pādapīḍanāsana[101]

39) Haṃsāsana[102]

40) Nābhītalāsana

41) Ākāśāsana

42) Utpādatalāsana

43) Nābhīlasitapādakāsana

44) Vṛścikāsana

45) Cakrāsana

46) Utphālakāsana

---

[95] HR2 3.51 calls the posture by its synonym Dhanurāsana.

[96] I follow here HR1 for the sake of consistency; compare similar names of postures, such as Bandhapadmāsana and Bandhamayūrāsana. HR2 reads Baddhamatsyendrāsana.

[97] The reading Kāndavāsana appears in the Kapālakuraṇṭakayoga cited in Reddy's footnote on p. 153 of his edition HR1.

[98] See HR2 3.69 for the full name of the *mudrā*.

[99] HR1 reads Yogamudrā.

[100] Also called Dhūnapīṭha in HR2 3.71.

[101] HR1 reads Pādapiṇḍana.

[102] HR1 reads Hiṃsāsana (misprint).

47) Uttānakūrmāsana

48) Kūrmāsana

49) Baddhakūrmāsana[103]

50) Nārjavāsana[104]

51) Kabandhāsana

52) Gorakṣāsana

53) Aṅguṣṭhāsana

54) Muṣṭikāsana

55) Brahmaprāsāditāsana

56) Pañcacūlikukkuṭāsana

57) Ekapādakukkuṭāsana

58) Ākāritakukkuṭāsana

59) Bandhacūlikukkuṭāsana

60) Pārśvakukkuṭāsana

61) Ardhanārīśvarāsana

62) Bakāsana

63) Dharāvahāsana

64) Candrakāntāsana

65) Sudhāsārāsana

66) Vyāghrāsana

67) Rājāsana

68) Indrāṇī-āsana

69) Śarabhāsana

70) Ratnāsana

71) Citrapīṭha

72) Baddhapakṣī-āsana

73) Īśvarāsana

74) Vicitranalināsana[105]

75) Kāntāsana

---

[103] The form Bandhakūrmāsana is not attested in the text, which otherwise uses the forms Bandhapadmāsana and Bandhamayūrāsana.

[104] Such a name is not attested in other texts. It is possible that *nārjava* was intended as a descriptive term meaning 'it is difficult.' However, such descriptive terms are not found elsewhere in this context.

[105] HR1 separates 74 into two postures, Vicitra and Nalina.

76) Śuddhapakṣī-āsana

77) Sumandrakāsana[106]

78) Caurangī-āsana

79) Krauñcāsana

80) Dṛḍhāsana

81) Khagāsana

82) Brahmāsana

83) Nāgapīṭha

84) Śavāsana

8.2 Jogapradīpakā, Section 3[107]

Different versions of the *āsana* names are recorded 1) in the text of the edition of the JP, which is a linguistically hybrid text, 2) in the English introduction to the JP by Gharote, 3) the captions of the line drawings appended to Gharote's edition (which correspond to the descriptions of the *āsanas* in another work by the same author, the Yogāsanamālā), 4) the inscriptions on the coloured drawings of manuscript Add. 24099 in the British Library, London, and 5) the accompanying text of that manuscript. In the left-hand column, I first list the names as they appear in section (*khaṇḍa*) 3 of Gharote's edition and add—in square brackets—variants of the names recorded in other parts of the book, including Gharote's English introduction. In the right-hand column I list the names of the *āsanas* as inscribed on the drawings of manuscript Add. 24099, followed by variants appearing in the text of the manuscript. In order not to burden the Appendix with too many minor orthographic variants, I have standardized the orthography somewhat by replacing the frequently used *anusvāra* with the class nasals.

1) Svastaka [Svastika] āsana	Svastika [Svastaka] āsana
2) Padma āsana (for the second variety, see 44)	Padmāsana
3) Netī āsana	Netī āsana
4) Udara āsana	Udara āsana
5) Saptariṣi [Saptarṣī/Saptarṣi] āsana	Saptariṣi āsana
6) Pūrva āsana	Pūrva āsana
7) Pachimatāṇa [Paścimatāṇa] āsana	Paścimatāṇa āsana
8) Vajrasaṃghāra [Vajrasinghāra/Vajrasiṃghāḍa] āsana	Vajrasinghāra āsana

[106] HR1 reads Sumandaka.

[107] I have transliterated the names following the edited hybrid text of the JP without attempting any corrections and Sanskritizations, since sufficient manuscript material was not available to me for comparison's sake. It is obvious that the edition also contains printing errors. In Hindī, unlike Sanskrit, the words *āsana* or *mudrā* following the names of postures are written as separate words.

9) Sūrya āsana	Sūrya āsana
10) Gorakhājālī/Gorakhajālī [Gorakhāñjali] āsana	Gorakhajālī āsana
11) Anasuyā [Anasūyā] āsana	Anasuyā [Anusūyā] āsana
12) Machandra [Machandar/Matsyendra] āsana (for the second variety, see 46)	Machendra āsana
13) Bhairū [Bhairava] āsana	Bhairū āsana
13a = 84) Sidhi/Sidha [Siddhi/Siddha] āsana	– (see 84)
14) Mahāmudrā āsana	Mahāmudrā āsana
15) Jonimudrā [Yonimudrā] āsana	Jonimudrā āsana
16) Mayūra āsana	Mayūra āsana
17) Kapālī [Kapāli] āsana	Kapālī āsana
18) Siva [Śiva] āsana	Siva āsana
19) Phodyā āsana	Phodyā āsana
20) Mākaḍa [Markaṭa] āsana	Mākaḍa āsana
21) Para āsana	Para āsana
22) Bhadragorakha āsana	Bhadragorakha āsana
23) Rūṇḍa [Ruṇḍa] āsana	Ruṇḍa āsana
24) Jogapada [Yogapada] āsana	Jogapada āsana
25) Cakrī āsana	Cakrī āsana
26) Ātamārāma [Ātamārāma] āsana	Ātamārāma [Ātamarāma] āsana
27) Mṛtyubhañjīka [Mṛtyubañjika/ Mṛtyubhañjika] āsana	Mṛtyubhañjīka āsana
28) Vṛścaka [Vṛścika] āsana	Vṛścika āsana
29) Viparītikarana [Viparītakaraṇa] āsana	Viparīta āsana
30) Deva āsana	Veda āsana
31) Gohī āsana	Gohī āsana
32) Kocaka āsana	Kocika āsana
33) Tapakāra āsana	Tapakara āsana
34) Bhiḍoka [Bhiṇḍoka] āsana	Bhiṇḍoka āsana
35) Brahmajurākusa [Brahmajurāṅkuśa] āsana[108]	Brahmajurāṅkusa āṣana
36) Andha āsana	Andha āsana

[108] See Brahmajvarāṅkuśāsana in Appendix 8.3, no. 19.

37) Bhiśrakā [Bhisarikā/Bhisarika/Bhisaraka] āsana	Miśrikā āsana
38) Aghora āsana	Aghora āsana
39) Vijoga/Viyoga āsana	Vijoga āsana
40) Joni [Yoni] āsana	Joni āsana
41) Bodhasoka āsana	Bodhasoka āsana
42) Bhaga [Bhāga] āsana	Bhaga āsana
43) Rudra āsana	Rudra āsana
44) Padma āsana (second variety; for the first variety, see 2)	Baddhapadmā āsana (= Baddhapadmāsana)
45) Sivaliṅga [Śivaliṅga] āsana	Sivaliṅga āsana
46) Machandra āsana (second variety; for the first variety, see 12)	Machindra āsana (second [*dutiya*] variety)
47) Vālamīka āsana	Vālamīka āsana
48) Vyāsa āsana	Vyāsa āsana
49) Dattadigambara āsana	Dattadigambara āsana
50) Sidhasamādhi [Siddhasamādhi] āsana	Siddhisamādhi āsana
51) Carapaṭacoka [Carapaṭacauka/Carpaṭacoka] āsana	Carapaṭacauka āsana
52) Gvālīpāva āsana	Gvālīpāu [Gvālīpāva] āsana
53) Kanerīpāva āsana	Katerīpāu āsana
54) Hālīpāva [Hālipāva] āsana	Hālīpāva āsana
55) Mīḍakīpāva āsana	Mīḍakīpāva āsana
56) Jalandhrīpāva [Jālandharīpāva] āsana	Jalandharīpāva āsana
57) Gopīcanda [Gopīcandra] āsana	Gopīcanda āsana
58) Bharatharī [Bhartṛhari] āsana	Bharatharī āsana
59) Vasiṣṭa [Vasiṣṭha] āsana	Vasiṣṭa āsana
60) Citra āsana	Citra āsana
61) Añjanī āsana	Añjanī āsana
62) Sāvatrī [Sāvitrī] āsana	Sāvitrī āsana
63) Garuḍa āsana	Garuḍa āsana
64) Sukadeva [Śukadeva] āsana	Sukadeva āsana
65) Nārada āsana	Nārada āsana
66) Narasiṃgha [Narasiṃha] āsana	Narasiṃgha āsana

67) Varāha āsana	Varāha āsana
68) Kapila āsana	Kapila āsana
69) Jatī [Yati] āsana	Yatī āsana
70) Vṛsapati [Vṛkṣa?] āsana	Vṛhaspati (= Bṛhaspati) [Vrahaspati] āsana
71) Pārvatī āsana	Pārvatī āsana
72) Kurkaṭa [Kurakaṭa?] āsana	Kukkuṭa āsana
73) Kākabhusaṇḍī [Kākabhṛsandi/ Kākabhuśuṇḍī] āsana	Kākabhuśuṇḍī āsana
74) Sidhaharatālī [Siddhaharatāli/Siddhahartālī] āsana	Siddhaharatālī āsana
75) Sumati āsana	Sumati āsana
76) Kalyāṇa āsana	Kalyāna (= Kalyāṇa) āsana
77) Urdhapavana [Ūrdhvapavana, Ūrdhvapayana] āsana	Urdhabhava āsana
78) Masaka [Maśaka] āsana	Masaka āsana
79) Brahma [Brahmā] āsana	Brahma āsana
80) Anīla [Anila] āsana	Anila āsana
81) Kūrma āsana	Kūrmāsana
82) Nagra [Nagara/Nagna] āsana	Nagna [Nagra] āsana
83) Parasarāma [Paraśurāma] āsana[109]	Parasarāma āsana
84) Sidhi/Sidha [Siddhi/Siddha] āsana	Siddha āsana

8.3 Hanūmān Śarmā 1935[110]

1) Siddhāsana
2) Prasiddhasiddhāsana
3) Padmāsana
4) Baddhapadmāsana
5) Utthitapadmāsana

[109] After the description of Parasarāma āsana JP repeats that of Sidhi/Sidha/Siddhi/Siddha āsana (see 13+).

6) Ūrdhvapadmāsana
7) Suptapadmāsana
8) Bhadrāsana
9) Svastikāsana
10) Yogāsana
11) Prāṇāsana
12) Muktāsana
13) Pavanamuktāsana
14) Sūryāsana
15) Sūryabhedanāsana
16) Bhastrikāsana
17) Sāvitrīsamādhi-āsana
18) Acintanīyāsana
19) Brahmajvarāṅkuśāsana
20) Uddhārakāsana
21) Mṛtyubhañjakāsana
22) Ātmārāmāsana
23) Bhairavāsana
24) Garuḍāsana[111]
25) Gomukhāsana
26) Vātāyanāsana
27) Siddhamuktāvalī-āsana
28) Neti-āsana
29) Pūrvāsana
30) Paścimottānāsana
31) Mahāmudrā
32) Vajrāsana
33) Cakrāsana
34) Garbhāsana
35) Śīrṣāsana

---

[110] The list of *āsanas* in Śarmā's article was adopted (with occasional small changes) in the publications by Daniélou 1949: 146–149 and Haṇmaṃte 1980: 553–554. Variant readings are indicated in the notes.
[111] Daniélou adds Siṃhāsana.

36) Hastādhāraśīrṣāsana[112]
37) Ūrdhvasarvāṅgāsana[113]
38) Hastapādāṅguṣṭhāsana
39) Pādāṅguṣṭhāsana
40) Uttānapādāsana
41) Jānulagnahastāsana[114]
42) Ekapādaśirāsana
43) Dvipādaśirāsana
44) Ekahastāsana
45) Pādahastāsana
46) Karṇapīḍamūlāsana[115]
47) Koṇāsana
48) Trikoṇāsana
49) Catuṣkoṇāsana
50) Kandapīḍāsana
51) Tulitāsana
52) Lolāsana, Tāḍāsana or Vṛkṣāsana[116]
53) Dhanuṣāsana
54) Viyogāsana
55) Vilomāsana
56) Yonyāsana
57) Guptāṅgāsana
58) Utkaṭāsana
59) Śokāsana
60) Saṃkaṭāsana
61) Andhāsana
62) Ruṇḍāsana[117]
63) Śavāsana
64) Vṛṣāsana

---

[112] Daniélou omits this *āsana*.
[113] Daniélou reads Sarvāṅgottānāsana.
[114] Daniélou reads Jānulagnāsana.
[115] Haṇmaṃte reads Karṇapīḍāsana.
[116] Haṇmaṃte reads only Vṛkṣāsana. Daniélou lists Lolāsana, Todāsana and Vṛkṣāsana.
[117] Haṇmaṃte reads Khaṇḍāsana.

65) Gopucchāsana
66) Uṣṭrāsana
67) Markaṭāsana
68) Matsyāsana
69) Matsyendrāsana
70) Makarāsana
71) Kacchapāsana[118]
72) Maṇḍūkāsana
73) Uttānamaṇḍūkāsana
74) Haṃsāsana
75) Bakāsana
76) Mayūrāsana
77) Kukkuṭāsana
78) Phodyāsana[119]
79) Śalabhāsana
80) Vṛścikāsana
81) Sarpāsana
82) Halāsana
83) Vīrāsana
84) Śāntipriyāsana

8.4 Gaṅgādharan Nair 1962[120]

1) Padmāsana
2) Baddhapadmāsana
3) Kārmukāsana
4) Siddhāsana
5) Baddhayonyāsana
6) Kṣemāsana
7) Muktāsana

---

[118] Daniélou reads Kacchāsana.
[119] Haṇmaṃte reads Padmāsana.
[120] The photographs of the postures in Nair's book could not be reproduced here because of their poor quality.

8) Guptāsana
9) Svastikāsana
10) Samāsana
11) Sukhāsana
12) Sūryāsana
13) Yogamudrā
14) Utthitapadmāsana
15) Ūrdhvapadmāsana
16) Kukkuṭāsana
17) Garbhāsana
18) Uttānakūrmāsana
19) Parvatāsana
20) Matsyāsana
21) Aṅguṣṭhāsana
22) Pakṣyāsana
23) Kākāsana
24) Bakāsana
25) Vīrāsana
26) Gomukhāsana
27) Ākarṇadhanurāsana
28) Ekapādakandharāsana
29) Vajrāsana
30) Suptavajrāsana
31) Marīcāsana
32) Dvipādakandharāsana
33) Dvipādabhujāsana
34) Ūrdhvapādaśīrṣāsana
35) Cakorāsana
36) Bāṇāsana
37) Upaviṣṭakoṇāsana
38) Paścimatāṇāsana
39) Jānuśīrṣāsana
40) Mahāmudram (!)
41) Gorakṣāsana

42) Bhadrāsana
43) Mayūrāsana
44) Ardhamatsyendrāsana
45) Pūrṇamatsyendrāsana
46) Kūrmāsana
47) Śaśakāsana
48) Vālivāmanāsana[121]
49) Maṇḍūkāsana
50) Śīrṣāsana
51) Śīrṣapadmāsana
52) Vṛkṣāsana
53) Siṃhāsana
54) Uṣṭrāsana
55) Tolāṅgulāsana
56) Bhujaṅgāsana
57) Śalabhāsana
58) Naukāsana
59) Dhanurāsana
60) Merudaṇḍāsana
61) Pavanamuktāsana
62) Halāsana
63) Kaṇṭhapīḍanāsana
64) Viparītakaraṇī mudrā
65) Sarvāṅgāsana
66) Ūrdhvapādahastāsana
67) Cakrāsana
68) Prasāritapādottānāsana
69) Pārśvottānāsana
70) Vīryastambhanāsana
71) Vātāyanāsana
72) Pādahastāsana
73) Uttānāsana

[121] One would have expected the reading Balivāmanāsana here.

74) Trikoṇāsana
75) Ardhacandrāsana
76) Ekapādāsana
77) Āñjaneyāsana
78) Vṛścikāsana
79) Pādāṅguṣṭhāsana
80) Upadhānāsana
81) Garuḍāsana
82) Vīrayogāsana
83) Yoganidrāsana
84) Uḍḍiyānabandha

8.5 Svāmī Svayamānanda 1992

1) Śavāsana
2) Padmāsana
3) Baddhapadmāsana
4) Bhujaṅgāsana
5) Śalabhāsana
6) Ardhaśalabhāsana
7) Dhanurāsana
8) Paścimottānāsana
9) Ardhapaścimottānāsana
10) Uttānapādāsana
11) Ardha-Uttānapādāsana
12) Halāsana (first variety)
13) Halāsana (second variety)
14) Sarvāṅgāsana
15) Ardhasarvāṅgāsana
16) Matsyāsana
17) Saralamatsyāsana
18) Vajrāsana
19) Suptavajrāsana

20) Śaśakāsana[122]
21) Ānandamadirāsana
22) Pādādirāsana
23) Siddhāsana
24) Baddhayoni-āsana
25) Matsyendrāsana
26) Ardhamatsyendrāsana
27) Pavanamuktāsana
28) Dvipādapavanamuktāsana
29) Gomukhāsana
30) Ākarṇadhanurāsana
31) Hanumānāsana
32) Mahāvīrāsana
33) Siṃhāsana (first variety)
34) Simḥāsana (second variety)
35) Uṣṭrāsana
36) Mayūrāsana
37) Yogamudrāsana
38) Tolāṅgulāsana/Tolāṅgalāsana
39) Tulāsana
40) Kukkuṭāsana
41) Haṃsāsana
42) Makarāsana
43) Bhṛṅgāsana
44) Śaśakāsana[123]
45) Kūrmāsana
46) Ardhakūrmāsana
47) Vṛścikāsana
48) Garuḍāsana
49) Cakrāsana
50) Ardhacakrāsana
51) Garbhāsana

[122] This *āsana* differs from 44, which bears the same name.

52) Parvatāsana
53) Kandharāsana
54) Jānuśirāsana
55) Vātāyanāsana
56) Pādahastāsana
57) Viparītapādahastāsana
58) Pādāṅguṣṭhāsana
59) Pādacālanāsana
60) Dvihastabhujāsana
61) Nābhidarśanāsana
62) Karṇapīḍāsana
63) Trikoṇāsana
64) Prāṇāsana
65) Utkaṭāsana
66) Saṃkaṭāsana
67) Setubandhāsana
68) Śīrṣāsana
69) Tāḍāsana
70) Yoganidrāsana
71) Viparītakaraṇīmudrāsana
72) Hastapādāsana
73) Hastapādāṅguṣṭhāsana (first variety)
74) Hastapādāṅguṣṭhāsana (second variety)
75) Prārthanāsana
76) Sthitaprārthanāsana
77) Ekapādāsana
78) Caraṇa-Uddhṛtāsana
79) Atipṛṣṭhanamitāsana
80) Koṇasaṃtulanāsana
81) Saṃtulanāsana
82) Samatvāsana

[123] This *āsana* differs from 20, which bears the same name.

83) Upaviṣṭāsana

84) Stūpāsana

8.6 The Yoga Challenge® System[124]

1) Vīrabhadrāsana (see photographs 1.1–1.3)

2) Sūryanamaskāra (see photographs 2.1–2.20)

3) Pārśvārdhacandrāsana (see photographs 3.1–3.2)

4) Ardhacandrāsana

5) Pādahastāsana

6) Trikoṇāsana

7) Daṇḍāyamānavibhaktapādajānuśirāsana

8) Utkaṭāsana (see photographs 8.1–8.3)

9) Garuḍāsana

10) Daṇḍāyamānajānuśirāsana

11) Daṇḍāyamānadhanurāsana

12) Tulādaṇḍāsana

13) Vibhaktahastatulādaṇḍāsana

14) Daṇḍāyamānavibhaktapādapaścimottānāsana

15) Tāḍāsana[125]

---

[124] The postures are listed as documented in a poster published in 2003. Initially the orthography was based on that found in an older typed list of ninety-one postures from Ghosh's College. This list does not include diacritical marks, contains some obvious typing mistakes and shows the influence of North Indian orthography. Upon request, I standardized and partially corrected the orthography of the *āsana* names for the poster publication. My corrections included, among others, the addition of diacritical marks and the replacement of the letter *b*, characteristic of North Indian orthography, by the letter *v*.

[125] The name of the *āsana* is transmitted without diacritical marks as 'Tadasana,' along with the translation 'tree posture' (see also Choudhury 2000: 91). Tāḍāsana is often translated as 'mountain posture' due to the influence of the translation of the name in B.K.S. Iyengar's book "Light on Yoga" (1984: 610). Iyengar shows a somewhat different Tāḍāsana, also known as Samasthiti. He derives the name of the posture from the word *tāḍa* ('mountain') attested only in Sanskrit lexicons. However, Sanchez's series already includes a mountain posture (Parvatāsana) as 35. I have previously conjectured that 'Tadasana' is a corruption of Tarvāsana (from: *taru* [tree] + *āsana* = *tarvāsana*) meaning 'tree posture.' Considering the common exchange between *ḍa* and *la* in Sanskrit and the fact that names of postures are often derived from local languages (*tāḍa* in Hindī means 'palm tree'), I now suggest that Tāḍāsana be understood as Tālāsana, meaning 'palm tree posture.' A 'palm tree posture' (*tāḍāsana*) is depicted in Yogeshwaranand Parmahansa 1987: 77, Dhirendra Brahmachari 1970: 179 with

16) Pādāṅguṣṭhāsana
17) Vāmanāsana
18) Khagāsana
19) Bakāsana
20) Aṅguṣṭhāsana
21) Prāṇāsana
22) Sukhāsana
23) Samāsana
24) Siddhāsana
25) Bhadrāsana
26) Svastikāsana
27) Ardhapadmāsana
28) Padmāsana
29) Utthitapadmāsana
30) Baddhapadmāsana
31) Tulāṅgulāsana
32) Garbhāsana
33) Matsyāsana
34) Makarāsana
35) Parvatāsana
36) Kukkuṭāsana
37) Śavāsana
38) Pavanamuktāsana (see photographs 38.1–38.2)
39) Bhujaṅgāsana
40) Śalabhāsana (see photographs 40.1–40.2)
41) Pūrṇaśalabhāsana

---

plates 104–105 and on several websites (see, for example, http://www.chennaionline.com/health/yoga/tadasana.asp, retrieved April 15, 2003). However, this posture differs in that the practitioner stands on the tips of his toes, stretching both arms upwards perpendicularly (see also Dharmasiṃha 1899, no. 34). In Yogeshwaranand Parmahansa's version, the practitioner's fingers are spread apart in a fan-like manner, reminiscent of the leaves of a palm tree. In the picture on the website, however, the fingers are interlocked and the palms turned upward. A variation of Tāḍāsana is documented in the Yoga Challenge® IV video. It corresponds to the posture commonly known as Vṛkṣāsana, where the practitioner stands on one leg with both arms raised high up. The list of ninety-one postures from Ghosh's College erroneously translates 'Tadasana' (15) as 'tree posture' and 'Brikkhasana' (91) as 'palm tree posture,' inasmuch as Tāḍāsana means 'palm tree posture,' and Vṛkṣāsana 'tree posture.'

42) Dhanurāsana

43) Suptavajrāsana

44) Ardhakūrmāsana

45) Uṣṭrāsana

46) Śaśakāsana

47) Jānuśirāsana

48) Paścimottānāsana

49) Vibhaktapādapaścimottānāsana

50) Maṇḍūkāsana

51) Utthitapaścimottānāsana

52) Pūrṇavibhaktapādajānuśirāsana

53) Ekapādarājakapotāsana

54) Daṇḍāyamānapūrṇajānuśirāsana

55) Naṭarājāsana

56) Ākarṇadhanurāsana

57) Catuṣkoṇāsana

58) Gomukhāsana

59) Ardhamatsyendrāsana

60) Ekapādagokilāsana

61) Ekapādaśirāsana

62) Dvipādaśirāsana

63) Utthitakūrmāsana

64) Kūrmāsana

65) Yoganidrāsana

66) Oṃkārāsana

67) Saṃkaṭāsana

68) Pūrṇabhujaṅgāsana

69) Pūrṇadhanurāsana

70) Pūrṇa-Uṣṭrāsana

71) Ūrdhvadhanurāsana

72) Ekapādaviparītadaṇḍāsana

73) Mayūrāsana

74) Baddhamayūrāsana

75) Ekapādamayūrāsana

76) Ekahastamayūrāsana
77) Halāsana
78) Sarvāṅgāsana
79) Ūrdhvasarvāṅgāsana
80) Śīrṣāsana
81) Ūrdhvaśīrṣāsana
82) Vyāghrāsana[126]
83) Vyāghrāsanavṛścikāsana[127]
84) Hastāsana

[126] Corrected from 'Bagghrasana.'
[127] Corrected from 'Bagghrasana-Brischikasana.'

Selected Bibliography and Abbreviations

Primary Texts[128]

Āgamarahasya. Ācāryaśrīsarayūprasādadvivedapraṇītam āgamarahasyam. 2 volumes (pūrvārddham, uttarārddham). Jodhpur: Rajasthan Oriental Research Institute, 1968–1969.

Amanaskayoga. Amanaska Yoga. Edited by B.M. Awasthi, English Translation by B. Singh. Delhi: Swami Keshawananda Yoga-Samsthan-Prakashana, 1987.

Aparokṣānubhūti. In: Complete Works of Sri Sankaracharya in the original Sanskrit. Volume 2: Miscellaneous Prakaranas. Madras: Samata Books, 1981 (revised edition): 215–233.

Aparokṣānubhūtidīpikā. Aparokṣānubhūtiḥ. Śrīparamahaṃsaparivrājakācāryyaśrīmacchaṅkarācāryyaviracitā paramahaṃsaparivrājakācāryyaśrīvidyāraṇyamuniviracitayā vyākhyayā samalaṅkṛtā. Śrījīvānandavidyāsāgarabhaṭṭācāryyeṇa saṃskṛtā prakāśitā ca. Kalikātānagara: Kalikātāyantra, 1897 (second edition).

Brahmasūtrabhāṣya by Śaṃkara. The Brahmasūtrabhāṣya. Text with Foot-Notes & Variants etc. Third Edition, Re-edited with Notes, Various Readings etc. by Nārāyan Rām Āchārya. Bombay: Nirṇaya Sāgar Press, 1948.

Dhyānabindu-Upaniṣad. In: The Yoga Upaniṣad-s with the Commentary of Śrī Upaniṣad-Brahmayogin. Edited by A. Mahadeva Sastri. Adyar, Madras: Adyar Library and Research Centre, 1968: 186–213.

GS Gheraṇḍa-Saṃhitā. Gheraṇḍa Saṁhitā. Edited by Swami Digambarji and M.L. Gharote. Lonavla: Kaivalyadhama S.M.Y.M. Samiti, 1997 (second edition).

GŚ Gorakṣaśataka. Gorakṣaśatakam (With introduction, text, English translation, notes

[128] The texts have been arranged in the order of the Roman (not the Sanskrit) alphabet to facilitate the use of the bibliography by non-specialists.

etc.). Critically edited by Svāmī Kuvalayānanda & S.A. Shukla. Lonavla: Kaivalyadhāma S.M.Y.M. Samiti, 1958, 1974 (reprint).

HP1 Haṭhapradīpikā. The Haṭhayogapradīpikā of Svātmārāma with the Commentary Jyotsnā of Brahmānanda and English Translation. Adyar, Madras: Adyar Library and Research Centre, 1975 (reprint of 1972).

HP2 Haṭhapradīpikā. Haṭhapradīpikā (with 10 Chapters) of Svātmārāma. With Yogaprakāśikā Commentary by Bālakṛṣṇa. Edited by M.L. Gharote and P. Devnath. Lonavla: The Lonavla Yoga Institute, 2001.

HR1 Haṭharatnāvalī. Hatharatnavali of Srinivasabhatta Mahayogindra. Editor: M. Venkata Reddy. Secunderabad: M. Ramakrishna Reddy, 1982.

HR2 Haṭharatnāvalī. Haṭharatnāvalī (A Treatise on haṭhayoga) of Śrīnivāsayogī. Critically edited by M.L. Gharote/P. Devnath/V.K. Jha. Lonavla: The Lonavla Yoga Institute, 2002.

Jīvanmuktiviveka. Jīvanmuktiviveka (Liberation in Life) of Vidyāraṇya. Edited with English Translation by S. Subrahmanya Sastri and T.R. Srinivasa Ayyangar. Adyar, Madras: Adyar Library and Research Centre, 1978 (revised edition).

The Treatise on Liberation-in-Life: Critical Edition and Annotated Translation of The Jīvanmuktiviveka by Vidyāraṇya by R.A. Goodding (unpublished doctoral dissertation, submitted to the Faculty of the Graduate School, University of Texas at Austin, 2002); retrieved December 17, 2003 from http:// www. robgoodd.net.

JP Jogapradīpakā. Jayatarāma kṛta jogapradīpakā. Edited by M.L. Gharoṭe. Jodhpur: Rajasthan Oriental Research Institute, 1999.

Maitrāyaṇīya-Upaniṣad. The Maitrāyaṇīya Upaniṣad: A Critical Essay, with Text, Translation and Commentary by J.A.B. van Buitenen. 'S-Gravenhage: Mouton & Co., 1962.

Mālinīvijayottaratantra. *See* Vasudeva 2004.

Mārkaṇḍeya-Purāṇa. The Mārkaṇḍeya-Purāṇa Translated with Notes by F.E. Pargiter. Delhi: Indological Book House, 1969 (reprinted from the 1904 edition published by the Baptist Mission Press, Calcutta).

N1 Nava nātha caurāsī siddha. <Compiled> by Yogī Naraharinātha. Vārāṇasī: Gorakṣa-nātha Maṭha, 1968 (in Hindī).

N2 Nava nātha caurāsī siddha bālāsundarī yogamāyā. Puṇe: Akhila Bhāratavarṣīya Yoga-pracāriṇī Mahāsabhā Prakāśanam, 1968 (in Marāṭhī).

Sāṃkhyasāra. Sāṁkhyasāra of Vijñānabhikṣu (Text and Translation with Notes) <by> Shiv Kumar. Delhi: Eastern Book Linkers, 1988.

Śārṅgadharapaddhati. Śārṅgadhara Paddhati. Being an Anthology of Sanskrit Verses Compiled by Śārṅgadhara. Edited by P. Peterson with an Introduction by S. Mukhopadhyaya. Delhi: Chaukhamba Sanskrit Pratishthan, 1987 (reprinted from the 1915 edition published by the Nirṇayasāgar Press, Bombay).

ŚS Śiva-Saṃhitā. The Siva Samhita. Translated into English by R.B.S. Chandra Vasu. New Delhi: Oriental Books Reprint Corporation, 1979 (third edition).

Tejobindu-Upaniṣad. In: The Yoga Upaniṣad-s with the Commentary of Śrī Upaniṣad-Brahma-yogin. Edited by A. Mahadeva Sastri. Adyar, Madras: Adyar Library and Research Centre, 1968: 45–115.

Tirumantiram. Tirumantiram: A Tamil Scriptural Classic by Tirumular. Tamil Text with English Translation and Notes by B. Natarajan. Mylapore, Madras: Sri Ramakrishna Math, 1991 (second impression).

Vasiṣṭha-Saṃhitā. Vasiṣṭha Saṁhitā (Yoga Kāṇḍa). Edited by Swami Digambarji/P. Jha/G.S. Sahay. Lonavla: Kaivalyadhama S.M.Y.M. Samiti, 1984 <second edition>.

Vāyu-Purāṇa. Mahāmuniśrīmadvyāsapraṇītaṃ vāyupurāṇam. Poona: Ānandāśrama, 1983.

Yogabīja. Yogabīja. Edited by R. Śrīvāstava. Gorakhpur: Gorakhnāth-Mandir, 1982.

Yogacūḍāmaṇi-Upaniṣad. In: The Yoga Upaniṣad-s with the Commentary of Śrī Upaniṣad-Brahmayogin. Edited by A. Mahadeva Sastri. Adyar, Madras: Adyar Library and Research Centre, 1968: 337–362.

Yogarāja-Upaniṣad. In: Un-published Upanishads. Edited by the Pandits of Adyar Library under the Supervision of C.K. Raja. Adyar: The Adyar Library (Theosophical Society), 1933: 1–3.

Yogasārasaṃgraha. Yoga-Sāra-Sangraha of Vijñāna-Bhikṣu. Translated by Ganganath Jha <accompanied by the Sanskrit Text>. New Delhi: Akay Book Corporation, 1986 (reprint).

Yogaśāstra of Dattātreya. Yoga Shastra of Dattatreya. Edited by B.M. Awasthi. Translated by A. Sharma. Delhi: Swami Keshawananda Yoga Institute, 1985.

Yogaśikhā-Upaniṣad. In: The Yoga Upaniṣad-s with the Commentary of Śrī Upaniṣad-Brahmayogin. Edited by A. Mahadeva Sastri. Adyar, Madras: Adyar Library and Research Centre, 1968: 390–463.

YS Yogasūtra(s). The Sāṁga Yogadars´ana or Yoga Dars´ana of Patañjali with the Scholium of Vyāsa and the Commentaries—Tattva Vais´ārdi, Pātañjala Rahasya, Yogavārtika and Bhāsvatī of Vācaspati Mis´ra, Rāghavānanda Sarasvatī, Vijñāna Bhikṣū & Hariharānanda Āraṇya. Edited with Introduction, Notes, Index, Appendices, etc. by Gosvāmī Dāmodara S´astrī. Benares: Jai Krishnaḍas-Haridas Gupta, 1935.

Yogatattva-Upaniṣad. In: The Yoga Upaniṣad-s with the Commentary of Śrī Upaniṣad-Brahmayogin. Edited by A. Mahadeva Sastri. Adyar, Madras: Adyar Library and Research Centre, 1968: 363–389.

Catalogues, Encyclopedias and Dictionaries

Blumhardt, J.F. 1899. Catalogue of the Hindi, Panjabi and Hindustani Manuscripts in the Library of the British Museum, London: British Museum.

Haṇmaṃte, S.S. 1980. Saṃkhyā-Saṃket Koś. Puṇe: Manohar Y. Jośī (third enlarged edition) (in Marāṭhī).

Leach, L.Y. 1995. Mughal and Other Indian Paintings from the Chester Beatty Library. Vol. II. London: Scorpion Cavendish Ltd.

Lokesh Chandra 1999–2005. Dictionary of Buddhist Iconography. New Delhi: International Academy of Indian Culture and Aditya Prakashan (15 volumes).

Mayrhofer, M. 1986–2001. Etymologisches Wörterbuch des Altindoarischen. 3 volumes. Heidelberg: Universitätsverlag C. Winter.

Mujumdar, D.C. 1950. Encyclopedia of Indian Physical Culture. Baroda: Good Companions.

New Catalogus Catalogorum. New Catalogus Catalogorum: An Alphabetical Register of Sanskrit and Allied Works and Authors. Edited by K. Kunjunni Raja. Volume 6. Madras: University of Madras, 1971.

Turner, R. L. 1966. A Comparative Dictionary of the Indo-Aryan Languages. London: Oxford University Press.

Secondary Sources

Alter, J.S. 1992. The Wrestler's Body: Identity and Ideology in North India. Berkeley: University of California Press.

Alter, J.S. 2000. Gandhi's Body: Sex, Diet, and the Politics of Nationalism. Philadelphia, Pennsylvania: University of Pennsylvania Press.

Alter, J.S. 2004. Yoga in Modern India: The Body between Science and Philosophy. Princeton, New Jersey: Princeton University Press.

Bernard, T. no date. Heaven lies within us. London: Rider, ca. 1939.

Bernard, T. 1938. Tantric Yoga (unpublished doctoral dissertation, submitted to the Faculty of Philosophy, Columbia University).

Bernard, T. 1939. Penthouse of the Gods: A Pilgrimage into the Heart of Tibet and the Sacred City of Lhasa. London: Scribner's Sons.

Bernard, T. 1944. Haṭha Yoga: The Report of a Personal Experience. New York: Columbia University Press.

Bhole, M.V./P. Jha/G.S. Sahay 1979. Asanas as an end and as a means in Yoga. Yoga Mimamsa 19: 46.

Bouy, C. 1994. Les Nātha-Yogin et les Upaniṣads: Étude d'histoire de la littérature hindoue. Paris: Édition-Diffusion de Boccard.

Brunner, H. 1994. The Place of Yoga in the Śaivāgamas. In: Pandit N.R. Bhatt Felicitation Volume. Edited by P.-S. Filliozat/S.P. Narang/C.P. Bhatta. Delhi: Motilal Banarsidass: 425–461.

Bühnemann, G. 2000–2001. The Iconography of Hindu Tantric Deities. Volume I. The Pantheon of the Mantramahodadhi. Volume II. The Pantheons of the Prapañcasāra and the Śāradātilaka. Groningen: E. Forsten.

Chidananda, Swami 1984. The Philosophy, Psychology and Practice of Yoga. Shivananda-nagar, Uttar Pradesh: The Divine Life Society.

Choudhury, B. (1978) 2000. Bikram's Beginning Yoga Class by Bikram Choudhury, with B.J. Reynolds, second edition edited by J. Goldstein. New York: J.P. Tarcher/Putnam (reprint).

Daniélou, A. 1949. Yoga: The Method of Re-Integration. London: Christopher Johnson.

Dasgupta, S. 1976. Obscure Religious Cults. Calcutta: Firma KLM Private Limited (reprint of the third edition of 1969; first edition published in 1946, revised in 1962).

Dave, M./M.V. Bhole 1987. Understanding the concepts of 'ha', 'sa', 'ṭha', and 'haṭha' in Yoga. Yoga Mimamsa 26: 26-46.

Desai, Yogi Amrit 1985. Kripalu Yoga. Meditation-In-Motion. Book II: Focusing Inward. Lenox, Massachusetts: Kripalu Yoga Fellowship.

Dharmasiṃha, Kahānjī 1899. Aṣṭāṅgayogāntargata sacitra cauryāyaśīṃ āsaneṃ. Muṃbaī: Karnāṭak Printing Press (in Marāṭhī).

Dhirendra Brahmachari 1970. Yogāsana Vijñāna: The Science of Yoga. Bombay: Asia Publishing House.

Ernst, C.W. 2003. The Islamization of Yoga in the Amrtakunda Translations. Journal of the Royal Asiatic Society 13: 199–226.

Feuerstein, G. 2002. 84 Āsanas. Retrieved May 17, 2002 from http://www.yrec. org/84_ asanas.html.

Gaṅgādharan Nair, K.P. 1962. Enpathinalu Yogāsanangal. 84 Yogāsanas (with 84 Photo Plates). Quilon (in Malayalam).

Gharote, M.L. 1985. Asanas – A Perspective. Yoga Mimamsa 24: 17–38.

Gharote, M.L. 1989. Asana: A Historical and Definitional Analysis. Yoga Mimamsa 28: 29–43.

Gharote, M.L. 1991. A Critical Note on Haṭhapradīpikā. Journal of the Oriental Institute (Baroda) 40: 243–248. [An almost identical version of the article with the same title appeared in Yoga Mimamsa 28 (1989): 17–28.]

Gharote M.L. 1991b. A note on Brahmananda, the commentator of Hathapradipika. Yoga Mimamsa 30: 80–83.

Gharote M.L. 1999. Yogic Techniques. Lonavla: The Lonavla Yoga Institute.

Gharote, M.M. 1998. Use of Yogic Practices by the Traditional Wrestlers in Mallapurāṇa. Yoga Mimamsa 33: 50–55.

Gode, P.K. 1940. Date of the Haṭhayogapradīpikā of Svātmārāma Muni. Indian Historical Quarterly 16: 306–313.

Goswami, S.S. 1959. Haṭha-Yoga: An Advanced Method of Physical Education and Concentration. London: L.N. Fowler & Co.

Grönbold, G. 1969. Ṣaḍ-Aṅga-Yoga: Raviśrījñāna's Guṇabharaṇī nāma Ṣaḍaṅgayogaṭippaṇī mit Text, Übersetzung und literarhistorischem Kommentar (unpublished doctoral dissertation, submitted to the Philosophische Fakultät, Ludwigs-Maximilians-Universität zu München).

Grönbold, G. 1983. Materialien zur Geschichte des Ṣaḍaṅgayoga I. Der Ṣaḍaṅga-yoga im Hinduismus. Indo-Iranian Journal 25: 181–190.
(English Translation: The Ṣaḍaṅgayoga in Hinduism. In: Grönbold 1996: 3–17.)

Grönbold, G. 1996. The Yoga of Six Limbs: An Introduction to the History of Ṣaḍaṅgayoga. Translated from the German by R.L. Hütwohl. Santa Fe, New Mexico: Spirit of the Sun Publications.

Grünwedel, A. 1916. Die Geschichten der vierundachtzig Zauberer (Mahāsiddhas) aus dem Tibetischen übersetzt. Baessler-Archiv: Beiträge zur Völkerkunde. Band 5, Heft 4/5. Leipzig/ Berlin: B.G. Teubner: 137–228.

Gupta, S./D.J. Hoens/T. Goudriaan 1979. Hindu Tantrism. Leiden: E.J. Brill.

Hirschi, G. 1997. Basic Yoga for Everybody: 84 Cards with Accompanying Handbook. York Beach, Maine: Samuel Weiser.
(Translation from the German: Lust auf Yoga. Freiburg im Breisgau: Hermann Bauer Verlag, 1997.)

Iyengar, B.K.S. 1984. Light on Yoga. London: Unwin Paperbacks (reprint).

Iyengar, B.K.S. 1989. The Tree of Yoga. Yoga Vṛkṣa. Edited by D. Rivers-Moore. Boston: Shambala, 1989.

Kokaje, R./M.L. Gharote 1981. A Note on the Words Haṭhayoga and Rājayoga. Journal of the Oriental Institute (Baroda) 30: 198–204.

Kuvalayananda, Swami 1926. The Rationale of Yogic Poses. Yoga Mimamsa 2: 207–217.

Linrothe, R. 2006. Holy Madness: Portraits of Tantric Siddhas. New York/Chicago: The Rubin Museum of Art and Serindia Publications.

Losty, J.P. 1985. The thousand petals of bliss: The Yoga force. Kos, Franco Maria Ricci (FMR) (American edition) 4 (Christmas)/17: 91–104, with 12 colour plates.

Losty, J.P. 1985b. Gli oggetti interiori: I mille petali della beatitudine. Kos, Franco Maria Ricci (FMR) (Italian edition) 2 (agosto-settembre)/16: 41–64, with 18 colour plates.

Michaël, T. 1993. La valeur libératrice de la prise de posture (*āsana*) dans le yoga classique. Les Cahiers de l'Herne 63 (Nirvāṇa): 138–157.

Michelis, E. de 2004. A history of Modern Yoga: Patañjali and Western Esotericism. London/ New York: Continuum.

Mittra, D. 2003. Asanas: 608 Postures. Novato, California: New World Library.

Mookerjee, A. 1971. Tantra. Hayward Gallery, London, 30 September – 14 November 1971 (second printing). London: Arts Council of Great Britain.

Nowotny, F. 1976. Das Gorakṣaśataka. Köln: R. Schwarzbold.

Pratinidhi, B. 1939. The Ten-Point Way to Health: Surya Namaskars. By Balasahib Pandit Pratinidhi, Raja of Aundh. Edited with an Introduction by L. Morgan. New York: D. Kemp Company.

Rastogi, N. 1992. The Yogic Disciplines in the Monistic Śaiva Tantric Tradition of Kashmir: Threefold, Fourfold, and Six-Limbed. In: Ritual and Speculation in Early Tantrism: Studies in Honor of André Padoux. Edited by T. Goudriaan. Albany, New York: State University of New York Press: 247–280.

Rawson, P. 1973. The Art of Tantra. Greenwich, Connecticut: New York Graphic Society Ltd.

Reck, C. 1997. 84 000 Mädchen in einem manichäischen Text aus Zentralasien? In: Bauddhavidyāsudhākaraḥ: Studies in Honour of Heinz Bechert on the Occasion of His 65th Birthday. Edited by P. Kieffer-Pülz and J.-U. Hartmann. Swisttal-Odendorf: Indica et Tibetica Verlag: 543–550.

Rinehard, R./T.K. Stewart 2000. The Anonymous Āgama Prakāśa: Preface to a Nineteenth-Century Gujarati Polemic. In: Tantra in Practice. Edited by D.G. White: Princeton, New Jersey: Princeton University Press: 266–284.

Robinson, J.B. 1979. Buddha's Lions: The Lives of the Eighty-Four Siddhas. Berkeley, California.

Śarmā, H. 1935. Yogavidyā: Āsan aur unkā upayog. Kalyāṇ 10. (September): 663–668 (in Hindī).

Satyananda Saraswati 1983. Surya Namaskara: A Technique of Solar Vitalization by Swami Satyananda Saraswati. Edited by Shankardevananda Saraswati. Munger: Bihar School of Yoga (third revised and enlarged edition).

Schmidt, R. 1908. Fakire und Fakirtum im alten und modernen Indien: Yoga-Lehre und Yoga-Praxis nach den indischen Originalquellen dargestellt. Berlin: Verlag von H. Barsdorf.

Sferra, F. 2000. The ṣaḍaṅgayoga by Anupamarakṣita with Raviśrījñāna's Guṇabharaṇī-nāmaṣaḍaṅgayogaṭippaṇī. Roma: Istituto italiano per l'Africa e l'Oriente.

Sjoman, N.E. 1999. The Yoga Tradition of the Mysore Palace. Delhi: Abhinav Publications (second revised edition).

Stenhouse, J. 2001. Sun Yoga: The Book of Surya Namaskar. <St. Christophe, France:> Innerspace Map Studio (self-published).

Svayamānanda, Svāmī 1992. Sacitra 84 yogāsan evaṃ svāsthya. Mathurā: Bhāṣā Bhavan (in Hindī).

Tucci, G. 1949. Tibetan Painted Scrolls. 2 volumes. Roma: La Libreria Dello Stato.

Unbescheid, G. 1980. Kānphaṭā: Untersuchungen zu Kult, Mythologie und Geschichte śivaitischer Tantriker in Nepal. Wiesbaden: Franz Steiner.

Vasudeva, S. 2004. The Yoga of the Mālinīvijayottaratantra: Chapters 1–4, 7, 11–17. Critical Edition, Translation & Notes. Pondichéry: Institut français de Pondichéry/École française d'extrême-orient.

Venkateshananda (†), Swami/A. Metcalfe/Acharya Upendra Roy 1984. Handbook of 84 Traditional Asanas (and 28 additional postures). No place: International Yoga Teachers' Association Inc.

Vivekananda, Swami (1896) 1978. Raja-Yoga or Conquering the Internal Nature. Calcutta: Advaita Ashrama (seventeenth impression).

White, D.G. 1996. The Alchemical Body: Siddha Traditions in Medieval India. Chicago: The University of Chicago Press.

White, D.G. 2003. Kiss of the Yoginī: "Tantric Sex" in its South Asian Contexts. Chicago: The University of Chicago Press.

Yogeshwaranand Parmahansa 1987. First Steps to Higher Yoga (An Exposition of First Five Constituents of Yoga). Delhi: Yoga Niketan Trust (third revised and enlarged English edition).

Index of Names of Āsanas Listed in the Appendices [129]

[129] To help non-specialists, the entries are arranged in the order of the Roman (and not the Sanskrit) alphabet. Numbers refer to the Appendices (8.1–8.6).

Baddhapakṣī-āsana 8.1/72
Baddhayonyāsana 8.4/5; 8.5/24
Bakāsana 8.1/62; 8.3/75; 8.4/24; 8.6/19
Bāṇāsana 8.4/36
Bandhacūlikukkuṭāsana 8.1/59
Bandhamatsyendrāsana 8.1/27
Bandhamayūrāsana 8.1/13 *see also* Baddhamayūrāsana
Bandhapadmāsana 8.1/6 *see also* Baddhapadmāsana
Bandhāsana 8.1/12
Bhadragorakha āsana 8.2/22
Bhadrāsana 8.1/2; 8.3/8; 8.4/42; 8.6/25
Bhaga/Bhāga āsana 8.2/42
Bhairavāsana 8.1/16; 8.3/23
Bhairū/Bhairava āsana 8.2/13
Bharatharī/Bhartṛhari āsana 8.2/58
Bhastrikāsana 8.3/16
Bhiḍoka/Bhiṇḍoka āsana 8.2/34
Bhiśrakā/Bhisarikā/Bhisarika/Bhisaraka/Miśrikā āsana 8.2/37
Bhṛṅgāsana 8.5/43
Bhujaṅgāsana 8.4/56; 8.5/4; 8.6/39
Bodhasoka āsana 8.2/41
Brahmajurākusa/Brahmajurāṅkuśa 8.2/35
Brahmajvarāṅkuśāsana 8.3/19
Brahmaprāsāditāsana 8.1/55
Brahmāsana 8.1/82; 8.2/79
Bṛhaspati āsana *see* Vṛsapati/Vṛkṣa (?)/Vṛhaspati (= Bṛhaspati)/Vrahaspati āsana

Cakorāsana 8.4/35
Cakrāsana 8.1/45; 8.3/33; 8.4/67; 8.5/49
Cakrī āsana 8.2/25
Candrakāntāsana 8.1/64
Cāndrāsana 8.1/29
Caraṇa-Uddhṛtāsana 8.5/78
Carapaṭacoka/Carapaṭacauka/Carpaṭacoka āsana 8.2/51

Garbhāsana 8.3/34; 8.4/17; 8.5/51; 8.6/32
Garuḍāsana 8.2/63; 8.3/24; 8.4/81; 8.5/48; 8.6/9
Gohī āsana 8.2/31
Gomukhāsana 8.1/21; 8.3/25; 8.4/26; 8.5/29; 8.6/58
Gopīcanda/Gopīcandra āsana 8.2/57
Gopucchāsana 8.3/65
Gorakhājālī/Gorakhajālī/Gorakhāñjali āsana 8.2/10
Gorakṣāsana 8.1/52; 8.4/41
Guptāṅgāsana 8.3/57
Guptāsana 8.4/8
Gvālīpāva/Gvālīpāu āsana 8.2/52

Halāsana 8.3/82; 8.4/62; 8.5/12; 8.5/13; 8.6/77
Hālīpāva/Hālipāva āsana 8.2/54
Haṃsāsana 8.1/39; 8.3/74; 8.5/41
Hanumānāsana 8.5/31
Hastādhāraśīrṣāsana 8.3/36
Hastapādāṅguṣṭhāsana 8.3/38; 8.5/73; 8.5/74
Hastapādāsana 8.5/72
Hastāsana 8.6/84

Indrāṇī-āsana 8.1/68
Īśvarāsana 8.1/73

Jalandhrīpāva/Jālandharīpāva āsana 8.2/56
Jānulagnahastāsana 8.3/41
Jānulagnāsana 8.3/41
Jānuśirāsana 8.5/54; 8.6/47
Jānuśīrṣāsana 8.4/39
Jatī/Yati/Yatī āsana 8.2/69
Jogapada/Yogapada āsana 8.2/24
Joni/Yoni āsana 8.2/40
Jonimudrā/Yonimudrā āsana 8.2/15

Mahāmudram (!) 8.4/40
Mahāvīrāsana 8.5/32
Mākaḍa/Markaṭa āsana 8.2/20
Makarāsana 8.3/70; 8.5/42; 8.6/34
Maṇḍūkāsana 8.1/23; 8.3/72; 8.4/49; 8.6/50
Marīcāsana 8.4/31
Markaṭāsana 8.1/24; 8.3/67 *see also* Mākaḍa āsana
Masaka/Maśaka āsana 8.2/78
Matsyāsana 8.3/68; 8.4/20; 8.5/16; 8.6/33
Matsyendrāsana 8.1/25; 8.3/69; 8.5/25
Mayūrāṣana (8.1/10–15;) 8.2/16; 8.3/76; 8.4/43; 8.5/36; 8.6/73
Merudaṇḍāsana 8.4/60
Mīḍakīpāva āsana 8.2/55
Mṛtyubhañjīka/Mṛtyubañjika/Mṛtyubhañjika āsana 8.2/27
Mṛtyubhañjakāsana 8.3/21
Muktāsana 8.3/12; 8.4/7
Muṣṭikāsana 8.1/54

Nābhidarśanāsana 8.5/61
Nābhīlasitapādakāsana 8.1/43
Nābhītalāsana 8.1/40
Nāgapīṭha 8.1/83
Nagra/Nagara/Nagna āsana 8.2/82
Nārada āsana 8.2/65
Narasiṃgha/Narasiṃha āsana 8.2/66
Nārjavāsana 8.1/50
Naṭarājāsana 8.6/55
Naukāsana 8.4/58
Neti-āsana 8.3/28
Netī āsana 8.2/3
Nirālambanāsana 8.1/28

Oṃkārāsana 8.6/66

Tulāsana 8.5/39
Tulitāsana 8.3/51

Udara āsana 8.2/4
Uddhārakāsana 8.3/20
Uḍḍiyānabandha 8.4/84
Upadhānāsana 8.4/80
Upaviṣṭakoṇāsana 8.4/37
Upaviṣṭāsana 8.5/83
Urdhabhava āsana *see* Urdhapavana āsana
Urdhapavana/Ūrdhvapavana/Ūrdhvapayana/Urdhabhava āsana 8.2/77
Ūrdhvadhanurāsana 8.6/71
Ūrdhvapādahastāsana 8.4/66
Ūrdhvapādaśīrṣāsana 8.4/34
Ūrdhvapadmāsana 8.3/6; 8.4/15
Ūrdhvasarvāṅgāsana 8.3/37; 8.6/79
Ūrdhvaśīrṣāsana 8.6/81
Uṣṭrāsana 8.3/66; 8.4/54; 8.5/35; 8.6/45
Utkaṭāsana 8.3/58; 8.5/65; 8.6/8
Utpādatalāsana 8.1/42
Utphālakāsana 8.1/46
Uttānakūrmāsana 8.1/47; 8.4/18
Uttānamaṇḍūkāsana 8.3/73
Uttānapādāsana 8.3/40; 8.5/10
Uttānāsana 8.4/73
Utthitakūrmāsana 8.6/63
Utthitapadmāsana 8.3/5; 8.4/14; 8.6/29
Utthitapaścimottānāsana 8.6/51

Vajrasaṃghāra/Vajrasiṅghāra/Vajrasiṃghāḍa āsana 8.2/8
Vajrāsana 8.1/3; 8.3/32; 8.4/29; 8.5/18
Vālivāmanāsana 8.4/48
Vālamīka āsana 8.2/47
Vāmanāsana 8.6/17

General Index[130]

Ādinātha, 13
Āgamaprakāśa, 13, 14
Āgamarahasya, 11, 13, 14
(*ajapā*) *gāyatrī*, 12
Amanaskayoga, 14, 15
Ambaragīra Yogin, 8
Amrit Desai, Yogi, 23
Amṛtakuṇḍa, 38
aṅga, 6ff.
Aparokṣānubhūti, 12, 13, 17, 19
Artistic Yoga Sport, 21
āsana, 1ff.,
āsanas on a rope, 21
āsanas on a wrestler's post, 21
aṣṭāṅganamaskāra, 32
aṣṭāṅgayoga, 6, 11, 15, 18, 23
Aṣṭāṅgayoga (of Pattabhi Jois), 22, 33
Atharvaveda, 5
Athletic Yoga, 21
Ātmārāma, 7

Bādarāyaṇa, 6
Bahr al-Hayat, 38
Bālakṛṣṇa, 7, 8
bandha, 15, 21, 30, 31, 143
Bernard, T., 24
Bhadrāsana, 25
Bhavanrao Pant (Raja of Aundh), 33
Bhojātmaja, 8
Bihar School of Yoga, 32
Bikram Choudhury, 31, 33
Bikram Yoga™, xi, 33, 34–35, 36
Bikram's Yoga College of India™, 33
Brahmānanda, 8, 17
Brahmasūtra(bhāṣya), 20
Buddhist, 18, 27

cakra, 7, 15
Caṇḍakāpāli, 8
Caugharā, ix, 86

Daniélou, 2, 29, 144, 154
Dasgupta, S., 26, 27, 85, 143
Dattātreya, 7, 14, 25
Deva āsana, 40
Dhyānabindu-Upaniṣad, 19
dṛṣṭi, 28

Galta, 9, 28
ghaṭa, 14
ghaṭa(stha)yoga, 14
Gheraṇḍa, 8

[130] This index does not include names of *āsanas* listed in the Appendices, which are indexed separately.